Psychic Generations:

A Gift Inherited

Cover design by ThomasMax (Lee Clevenger/R. Preston Ward)

Edited by Lee Clevenger

ISBN-13:   978-0-9799950-6-4
ISBN-10:   0-9799950-6-x

First printing, September, 2008

Published by:

Published by:

ThomasMax Publishing
P.O. Box 250054
Atlanta, GA 30325
404-794-6588
www.thomasmax.com

Psychic Generations

A Gift Inherited

Mildred Martin Cooley

ThomasMax

Your Publisher
For The 21st Century

ACKNOWLEDGMENTS

A special thanks to my husband Pete for all his encouragement and patience.

Also, a heartfelt thanks to my sister Ann for all the time she devoted to typing my book. She spent many hours correcting my spelling and learning about my strange life. Love her forever!

Many thanks to my very loving, wonderful family and friends who have been so supportive and have given me permission to use their names.

I would like to express my gratitude to Dr. Raymond Cook for his help in editing my book.

And, a special thanks to my granddaughter, Mary Rebecca Warbington Wells, for helping me achieve completion of my dream.

This book is dedicated to my family:
past, present, and future

TABLE OF CONTENTS

PREFACE

My father sent a message to me from the grave:
"FINISH YOUR BOOK"

The morning of February 26, 1981, was unusually warm. It was going to be an early spring that year. The camellias, azaleas, and narcissus were already in full bloom. "I must remember to take some flowers to the nursing home today," I thought.

My father was 86 years old. He had been in the hospital, critically ill, for quite a while. However, he had gotten strong enough to go to a nursing home. My mother and I went every day to be with him. He wouldn't say much. He would just sit there smiling, his beautiful blue eyes twinkling.

When I'd go in his room I'd always say, "Daddy, do you know who I am?"

He would then reassure me by answering, "Yes, darling, you're my baby daughter."

Every morning when we would go through this little ritual and his roommate appeared so disgusted and would grumble under his breath, "Don't look like a baby to me," as he shuffled out into the corridor. Then we would all have a little laugh.

On my way to the car I picked a beautiful bouquet of flowers from my yard and arranged them in a small white vase. They were so beautiful that I could hardly wait to surprise Daddy. He loved the sweet aroma of the narcissus. When Mother and I arrived at his room, we were stunned to find him slumped over in his chair, hardly breathing and semi-conscious. Frantically, we summoned the nurses and they tried to stabilize him until the ambulance came. There wasn't much time left for him after we got to the hospital. Only long enough to kiss him goodbye and tell him for the last time how much we loved him. Then I held his hand until he slipped into the next world.

Several days later we went to collect his belongings and there sat the little vase of flowers that he never got to see.

Daddy

A few weeks later, after everything had settled down, Mother and I were making one of our weekly trips to check on his grave. For the first time since he died I took fresh flowers from my yard for him. That same night as I went to bed, I was in the dozing-off state, visualizing that I was at the cemetery fixing Daddy's flowers. When I stood up and started to walk away I heard a quiet voice beckon to me, "Baby." I turned around only to find my Daddy smiling, standing next to his tombstone. He had on the same navy-blue suit in which he had been buried. He looked handsome standing there with his snow-white hair and blue eyes. As I looked at him he said, "Thank you for the flowers, darlin'." It made me so happy that I was able to see him again even though it was in this manner. I felt from that moment on that he was with me constantly.

Several months later I decided to go to a psychic for a reading. I had been to Emil Trammer before. She is very well known in the Southeast. She had no knowledge of my father's death. However, during the reading she said a spirit that had not been on the other side for long was trying to send me a message. Then she described Daddy in great detail, even to his beautiful blue eyes. The message he sent to me was, "Finish your book, baby daughter."

So it is in his honor and memory I have taken pen in hand and set out to do as he wished . . . .

CHAPTER 1

INTRODUCTION

If only you could be here with me now in my living room so I could tell you my story informally over a cup of hot coffee. You will soon find out that I am not a professional writer. I do not have a vocabulary of very fancy adjectives and adverbs. I have always enjoyed the simple things in life and conversation is generally the same, plain and direct.

Let me tell you something about myself. I am a 5' 3", 128-pound, blond-haired, blue-eyed, very happy, sensible, Christian woman who adores children. I immensely enjoy the profession of Kindergarten Teacher in a wonderful church school. My God and my family are always first in my life. Although we are a family of average means I have always felt very rich in blessings.

A neighbor who had seen an electric organ delivered to our home had made the comment that we must be rich to afford this luxury. My oldest daughter, Kathleen, who was 14 at that time, jumped right in and informed her, "Yes, ma'am, we're rich all right but not in money; our family is rich with love." My heart nearly burst with pride!

We have always opened our home to everyone and generally enjoyed the Grand Central Station atmosphere. Our evening meal has always been the focal point of the day and the most treasured of moments to me. The family all gathered around for the sharing of our events of the day. Problems settled, jokes swapped, happy conversation and, for the most part, the love there always seemed so over-whelming. I could write another book on all the wonderful people who have shared our good ol' red rice, collards, fried chicken and hush puppies!

There always seemed to be room for extra plates on our dinner table. The different experiences I am about to relate to you can be verified by most of my family and many of our friends, who have shared the majority of the spine tingling occurrences.

When I was a very young girl I can remember well my father telling me all about his grandmothers and how they were both gifted in a psychic sort of way. They never really talked about it except to my father. After all, a hundred years ago, possessing a psychic gift was a forbidden subject. My daddy recalled to me some of the things they had told him. The gift was passed from them to him.

Daddy used to read tea leaves for people. The story I liked best was about the time my parents were first married. They moved from Georgia to Chicago. One night, Mil and Gene, their friends, invited them over to their apartment for supper. As they sat around the table enjoying a tasty meal, the doorbell rang. Gene's neighbor barged in and walked straight over to Daddy and demanded, "I understand you read tea leaves! Is that right?"

"Well, yes I do," Daddy replied, totally taken aback by the man's rudeness.

"Well, if you are so damn smart, read mine," he said as he shoved a tea cup, empty except for a few tea leaves, into my father's face.

My father was very cool. He calmly took the cup from this man he'd never met. Then, after studying for a few minutes replied, "Within two weeks you will have a surprise visit from a man that will be wearing a white Panama straw hat and you will be very happy to see him. Also, before the last snow you will receive a telegram telling you about the death of someone close to you, so prepare yourself."

The neighbor thrust his head back and with a smart-aleck laugh, told my father he was crazy because "It is only the first week of March and the snow is still falling, so no one in Chicago would wear a white straw hat this time of the year." He turned abruptly on his heels and marched out of the apartment. Gene and Mil were quite embarrassed. Gene explained that the day before they had been bragging on Daddy's psychic ability but never dreamed their neighbor would be so discourteous. Everyone laughed about it and went on with the meal.

Several weeks later Gene stopped by the factory where Daddy worked. "Leon, I have a message for you from my neighbor. He said to tell you that his brother-in-law came from Alabama and surprised them. When they opened the door he was standing there in a white Panama straw hat. It is already spring-like weather in the south," he explained, "and everybody was already wearing light clothes. His brother-in-law did not realize it was still cold and snowing in Chicago and he felt quite foolish. Also, my neighbor had received a telegram that his mother had passed away and asked me to apologize to you."

When I was growing up I used to beg Daddy to read my tea leaves but he never would. I couldn't understand why so Mother told me that one day he had read his own leaves and appeared to be very upset. He put his cup down firmly and said, "I'll never ever read again for anybody." And he didn't.

I have always thought how wonderful it would have been if my grandmothers and Father would have written down all of their experiences to pass on to their heirs. Perhaps if I could have understood in the beginning that I had a gift passed to me from God through my ancestors I would not have been so afraid and would have possibly done so much more than just dabble in it all. I would have, at this point in my life, cherished and appreciated so much having knowledge of their experiences. It is mainly for this reason that I started writing this book for my grandchildren. I already know that all five of them have this gift. They each bear the *Cross La Mystic* (Psychic Cross) on their palms.

CHAPTER 2

IN THE BEGINNING

I really cannot remember when all of my psychic experiences started because I was not aware of the gift God placed on me for a long time. Most people have, at some time or another, had peculiar, weird or coincidental things happen to themselves and wondered if it was ESP, *déjà-vu*, or just a by-chance thing. Perhaps this is what I felt too when I began having visions. I am not completely precise in this thought, as for awhile it was all funny. Then, as more of the visions occurred I was baffled and later even afraid.

Retreating back as far as my memory would allow and still be accurate, in search for the beginning, I recall a particular night in the fall of 1956. My husband, Pete, had gone on a business trip up North for the refinery at which he was employed. My two oldest daughters, Kathleen and Madeline, who were, respectively, age six and three at the time, shared a bedroom. Each in their own little twin beds, they were tenderly kissed and tucked in for the night. Their last regular request was, "Mommy, please lie down by us for a little while." Well, what extremely tired mother could deny such a simple request? Especially if the mother was a very scary type of person that didn't particularly want to sleep in her own bedroom alone anyway. With their "dear-ol' Dad" not home, we slept with all the lights on and all the doors barricaded, not really knowing of what we were afraid.

Having set my clock and placed it on the bedside table, I snuggled up to my younger daughter Madeline, in whose bed I was resting on at that time, while I held hands with Kathleen between the beds. Sometime later, in the drifting off to sleep period, a vision beyond belief appeared to me. It was *Jesus in all His glory.* In a burst of brilliant yellow light, he appeared in white robes, his hands extended up. He said nothing. He just looked at me, standing there in overwhelming form. He stood there for a few minutes, then vanished. I lay there for a moment stunned, trembling, frightened and suddenly aware that my entire body was drenched in a cold, clammy sweat. I quickly got up and looked at the bed. There was a wet outline of my entire body, arms legs and head. My gown was wet. It was incomprehensible why Jesus would show himself to me. What did this mean? All kinds of thoughts crossed my mind. Maybe I was going to die? I had heard of people having religious experiences just before death. Needless to say, I did not sleep the rest of the night, which seemed never-ending.

Oh, for the first glorious ray of sunlight!

When Pete came home the next morning, I met him excitedly at the door and told him what had happened. He reassured me and told me not to worry . . . that maybe Jesus was trying to tell me He loved me and would take care of me and for me not to be afraid.

I will always believe it was at this particular instant that God entrusted this gift to me.

I can vaguely remember a few visions occurring after that night that did not have any significant meaning so we would laugh and chalk it up as coincidence. At this time I did not have the ability to interpret the sighting accurately. The first time I realized there was a message behind the visions, it frightened me a little.

I recall one morning, after putting the water on for coffee, I plopped back into bed to await the shrilling sound of the whistling water kettle. After closing my eyes, my family appeared in my "mind's eye." We were getting into our automobile and as I started the motor I realized that there was a maroon-colored car parked in front of ours. The man in the driver's seat I recognized as being my father. Knowing he had a blue car, I assumed that he had bought a new car. So I jumped out of our car and ran up to Daddy only to find that he had slumped over the steering wheel, dead. Startled, I opened my eyes and bounced out of bed, trying to shake this image out of my mind. My father worked out of town and commuted back and forth on the weekends. Well, today was the day he was to be home. At noon, his regular time of arrival, I phoned my mother to ask if he had arrived home. Getting a negative answer, I called repeatedly until 3:00 in the afternoon. Frantic, I decided to go over and wait with her. As I was telling her what I had seen, Daddy drove up. He apologized for being late but told us he had to go to a funeral. A man he worked with had died. Now, first off, my father never goes to funerals. He always prefers to remember his friends as he last saw them. Analyzing the matter, I figured Daddy appearing to be dead represented funeral or death. But why the maroon car? I asked him if he drove his car to the funeral and her replied that a friend of his had just purchased a new car and wanted him to ride with him. Do I have to tell its color? Maroon, of course.

During the course of this book I will refer to myself as having "just lain down." You must understand that most of my visions occurred at night when I retired to bed. It seems when my body begins to relax and my thoughts are fading, I am most receptive to these visions.

Another evening in September 1968, after retiring, I saw an old woman wearing wire-rimmed glasses, smiling a very toothy smile. I sat up in bed and told Pete, my very patient husband, about it. I sent my children for a pencil and paper. I drew the lady's picture as well as my artistic abilities allowed. After everyone laughed about it, I hurried the children back to bed. As soon as I lay back down and closed my eyes, another vision appeared. It was so funny that I burst out laughing almost uncontrollably. Pete inquired as to what could possibly be so funny this late at night. So I told him I saw a man feeding chickens. Having always been a city girl, this was really funny to me. Why would I see chickens? Well, that was really the joke of the night. Early the next morning as I was busying myself in the kitchen, the children rushed up to me with the morning newspaper. They thrust a picture in my face and very excitedly said, "Mother, here is your old lady." Well, it sure was . . . toothy smile and all.

Awed by this we went through the day thinking, "We found the old lady, now what about the chickens?" When the mailman came, we received a letter from my sister, Ann, who lives 300 miles away in Orange City, Florida. Her husband is a contractor and land developer, and she works in the office as his secretary. In her letter she announced that they had just bought a new business as an investment. You guessed it: a chicken business!

In my earlier years, I spent many enjoyable afternoons as leader of a Girl Scout troop. The girls took turns providing the refreshments each week. They came to the meeting place directly from school and were always famished. I was hurrying around the house getting ready to go to the meeting when suddenly a wave of panic swept over me as a thought rushed into my mind: Karen was going to forget the refreshments. This child was crippled and very self-conscious of her handicap. She was very intelligent and not absent-minded one bit; so why should this feeling persist within me? Karen had been so exuberant that it was her turn to serve and feel important. Even with all these thoughts racing through my head, I could not shake the feeling. I knew that sweet little girl would be embarrassed to tears. So, I planned a course of action that would help her, if need be. I took some Kool-Aid and a package of cookies from my refrigerator, placed them in a bag, threw them in the car and dashed to the meeting. When the girls arrived I prepared them by telling them, "If Karen forgets the refreshments, remember that a good Girl Scout is kind, so don't make her feel bad."

About that time the door burst open and a precious round, smiling face completely out of breath dashed up to me and blurted out, "Guess what, Mrs. Cooley? Mama and I got almost here before I remembered the refreshments. But we hurried back to the store and here they are, see!" She held the big bag high over her head in a victorious manner. Secretly thanking the Lord for stimulating her memory, I gave her a big hug of approval as all the girls broke into a round of applause upon seeing ice-cream sandwiches.

Another time we were going on a field trip. As the girls came in, they gave me their permission slips and jokingly I would read them out loud. One scout named Susan stood there quietly waiting her turn. Then she asked, "Guess what I have?"

Taking her envelope and trying to think of the most ridiculous thing I could imagine, I said, "A thousand-dollar bill." Her sweet little face suddenly drained of all color. I opened the envelope and to my surprise discovered an old, dirty, faded-out Confederate $1,000 bill (an advertisement).

The next day, in my twilight state, I saw an old woman rubbing the back of her head. Twenty-four hours later I was called to my grandmother's home for an emergency. She had had a stroke and could hardly speak. When the doctor arrived, he ordered an ice bag to be put on the same part of her head that I had seen the old lady rubbing. He said the clot was from within that particular area.

As summer was coming to an end, various school clubs hurried to plan one last beach party. Our oldest daughter, Kathleen, was a member of the local high school's Girls Athletic Association. They were having one last weekend fling of swimming and getting blistered by the sun before school began. The night before we were to go pick her up, I saw a vision of the ocean calm and glistening, rolling on the shore very softly. No waves with it, just like glass. I had a feeling that something was wrong. Pete assured me that I would have heard if there had been. Without another thought about the vision I went to sleep. When we arrived at the beach the next morning the ocean was as I saw in my vision, calm and glassy. Then we met a very excited Kathleen telling us about two of her girlfriends that had rented floats and paddled out into the surf. They just lay there, drifting around for awhile, not realizing that they were drifting out to sea. When they tried to get off the floats they were way over their heads and neither could swim. So they panicked and started screaming. No lifeguards were available so two of the other girls that could swim dashed in to pull the floats ashore. But they didn't realize either, in this unusually still ocean, how deep they were out. Then the ultimate thing happened. The treacherous undertow, the changing of tides, began. At high tide when it starts to go out, it has a terrific suction on anything in the water. With all four girls now in trouble, we all stood there helpless as some of the girls had run down the beach to find lifeguards. It took six professional lifeguards to pull the stranded girls safely ashore from the strong clasp of the ocean. After this near-tragic occurrence we helped the chaperones, still nervous wrecks, pack up all the kids and send them home.

Several weeks later, I had just lain down to go to sleep when in my mind's eye I saw two figures in detail, but they were in silhouette form. The smaller figure dropped to the ground as the larger figure hovered. I could see a knife being thrust into the smaller person that was lying on the ground. This really scared me. The next day my mother, who worked for a local florist, called to tell me about some acquaintance of ours that lived in North Carolina. They had a seven-year-old daughter who, the night of my vision, had been raped by a next-door neighbor and then stabbed to death. She had been left on her own front porch to die.

A cousin of my husband's had a brand new, yellow Cadillac. I saw in my twilight state her windshield being crushed by a case of Coca Cola bottles only to hear that the next day she was passing a "Coke" truck, lost control of her new car and hit a tree. Her head hit the windshield and she sustained a fractured skull.

Not far from our home is a very well-kept church cemetery. We pass by this cemetery almost every day. In its history there has never been a drainage problem. So, I really do not know why I should have made a remark like I did that day. But as the family was riding by this property in pouring rain, my youngest daughter, Mary Anne, said, "Mother, how would you like to live there?" She was referring to a house whose back yard was flooded, the yard's back fence next to a brand-new grave.

"I wouldn't want to live there and have some casket come floating up in my backyard," I laughed. Everyone else laughed too, except Pete, who gave me a disgusted look. The next afternoon when we rode by and saw the casket from the week-old grave, it had indeed floated up to the surface and was sitting above ground right at that yard's back fence.

"Mother, don't you ever say anything else like that again because it might happen," demanded my family.

Believe me . . . I did watch what I said for a long time after that!

CHAPTER 3

AUNT RUTH

Several peaceful months passed with only normal happy everyday things going on. It was Madeline's birthday and we had our usual birthday party, with all her friends and our family. After a great evening when all the guests had gone, I cleaned up the mess and happily, but tiredly, I climbed into bed and snuggled up to Pete, who was reading a book. As I lay there a picture came to my mind's eye. As I tried to focus in it clearer, I saw a woman far, far away. She was walking through some double swinging doors. I thought to myself "I wonder who that is?" I could see her gray coat; a kerchief was around her head, and her hands were in her pockets. As she got closer to my mind's eye, she was larger and then I could see her face clearly. She smiled at me and the sudden realization came: "That's me." As I lay there looking at myself I saw my face starting to blur out. In its place was a spinning, swirling type motion. It went round and round and round, then it started slowing down. When it finally came back into focus, where my face had been was a skull. I screamed and sat up hysterically and cried, "Honey, I must be going to die!" I related my reasoning to Pete. He put his book down, put his arms around me, and kissing me tenderly on the forehead, he reassured me not to worry as long as I felt good.

Well, I really did feel fit as a fiddle! It took hours though before I could get to sleep. At this point, I resolved never to close my eyes again. I would sit up in the bed every night until I fell hard and fast asleep, then there could be no time for clairvoyance. Of course, you know how many nights that lasted.

The very next morning at 7:30 I was trying to get the children ready for school when the telephone rang. It was my mother. She told me that my Aunt Ruth had been in an accident and had been taken to Memorial Hospital. Mother had no car to go see Ruth, so she asked would I please hurry to the hospital and see what I could find out. Aunt Ruth had always been very special to me.

Observing the rain outdoors, I threw my gray raincoat over my shoulders, tied my kerchief under my chin and ran to the car, cautioned by the family to drive careful in the rain.

I did not realize until sometime later that the vision I had the night before was unfolding before my eyes.

As I opened the hospital's double swinging doors and walked down the long corridor to the emergency room, I saw Ruth's son, Irvin, in the waiting room, and as I approached him I said "How is your mother?"

He replied, "Okay, I guess. They haven't told me anything yet."

We stood there for a few minutes visiting with a distant cousin who happened to be passing by when Ruth had the accident. The nurse came and asked if one of us would like to go in and stay with her in the emergency room. Irvin looked at me and pleaded "Would you please go in? Things like this make me nervous."

"Sure," I replied and hustled down the hall with the nurse to the small, quiet examining room. There she lay, so still on the table. I walked over to her and took her hand "Ruth," I said, "it's Mildred, can you hear me?" She blinked her eyes open, straining to see me, and without a sound she tenderly squeezed my hand. The silence was so prevailing; the whole scene seemed morbid. I leaned over her, brushing her hair off her face, I kissed her cheek softly and whispered, "I love you, Ruth."

She opened her eyes and tried to speak but could barely garble out, "I love you too." Those were the last words she ever spoke to me as she soon lapsed into a coma.

The family doctor called in a neurologist who happened to be in the hospital. When he came in to examine her, he told me that I did not have to leave. So I stood at the head of the table, still holding her hand, watching. "I thing she has had a stroke," he stated. At that point he took a tiny, powerful miniature flashlight from his pocket, and as he placed this in Ruth's mouth he instructed the nurse to turn off the lights in the room. This threw the room into pitch-black darkness. When I looked down at her face, I almost fainted. I could see her skull in its entirety, just as it had been in my vision, when the picture of my face had turned into a skull. It was at that moment I knew she would die, because that was the feeling I had had last evening, and generally the feelings I received with the visual impressions were accurate.

The next day I was in the room with Irvin, and we watched her die. The nurse, standing by the bed, shouted for me to summon the resident surgeon on the double. But the floor supervisor was so darn pokey that upon my return to Ruth's room, I almost ran into a man I recognized as a doctor. "Please come in here quick," I pleaded. "My aunt is dying, we think; please help her."

Dashing past the few nurses that had rushed into her room, he quickly took charge. After listening to her heart he spontaneously began pounding her chest with his clenched fist, then administered continuous heart massage. Interrupting the pace after a few minutes, he again listened for her heartbeat to no avail. Again he frantically pounded and massaged for a short while longer. The atmosphere was tense as the doctor once again searched for her heartbeat. Smiling, he nodded to us as he gave the nurse some directions.

However, two days later, just as I arrived at the hospital I met Irvin coming out of her room. "Mothers gone," he said tearfully. Quietly I walked to her bedside. She couldn't die . . . she was only fifty-four years old and I could not stand the thought of never seeing her again. I had never touched a dead person before, and had always sworn that I never would. But before I realized it, once again as I had in the emergency room, I was brushing her hair off her brow and kissing her cheek. "I love you, Ruth." *Oh, God, she can't hear me, she will never ever know how much I loved her.* That bothered me for a long time.

All I could recall in my grief was a poem my daddy used to quote to people, then he'd say, "If you can't send me flowers while I am alive, don't send them to me when I am dead." I would like to share this poem from an unknown author and my new-found philosophy.

If with pleasure you are viewing anything a man is doing,
If you like him or you love him tell him now.
Don't withhold the approbation 'til a parson makes oration,
And he lies with snowy lilies on his brow.
For no matter how you shout it, he won't really care about it,
He won't care how many tear drops you have shed.
So if you think some praises is due to him, now's *the time to slip it to him,*
For he cannot read his tombstone when he's dead.
More than fame and more than money, is a comment kind and sunny,
Or the hearty, warm approval of a friend.
And it adds to life a Savor, makes you stronger, braver,
And gives you heart and courage to the end.
So don't wait till life if over and he's underneath the clover,
For you cannot read your tombstone when you're dead.

Ruth adored children and was so good to us! She would borrow Grandpa's old Model-T Ford (named "Henry") and take us to picnics, beach, movies and even to the cemetery to rake all the family plots. Then we would go to the river bluff and have a piece of watermelon while we watched the shrimp boats go by. In my eyes she was great! And the extreme love and devotion I, myself, have for children today, is but a reflection of her kindness and generosity shown to all us kids.

About a week after the funeral, Irvin phoned to ask if I could possibly help him and his wife, Roberta, dispose of some of Ruth's belongings. I agreed, and the next day we found ourselves bewildered at so many duplicated items. She literally never threw anything away. I believe she had every piece of clothing she ever bought. There were clothes ranging from sizes 9 thru 16. She had under-panties from sizes 5 to 40! There were pink short panties, pink long panties, pink short with lace, pink with no lace in virtually every size. There were pink poka dots, purple dotted, black lace, black plain, long, short, bikini in every color and size. We laughed and laughed, and actually counted 132 pairs. Bras and slips were the same story, half slips any color and any size . . . long ones and evening ones. We counted 57 pairs of shoes, I kid you not! We ended up outfitting almost everybody in the family. We knew Ruth was probably right there with us and laughing as hard as we were. I bet she never realized what a collector she was!

After we organized the clothing we went into the kitchen. Now this was really strange. At random, Irvin pointed out five different appliances and asked directly, "Do you want this toaster and waffle iron? I don't need them."

"Well, I sure do, thanks," I answered.

"How about this mixmaster and wall clock?" he inquired.

"Golly Moses," I responded, "How did you know what I needed? Thanks a bunch," I said as he slipped a new electric iron in my box. *I'm not believing this,* I thought to myself. What was so weird, given the many appliances in the kitchen, I was offered exactly the things I needed. In the past several weeks, my toaster, iron, waffle iron, clock and mixmaster had all gone on the blink, and we couldn't afford to buy new ones. I will always feel that Ruth was there with us, pointing out to him the things she knew I needed so bad.

One night shortly after everything had settled down, Ruth came to me in a dream. She wore an antique-looking dress and a large black picture hat. She smiled at me and said, "Don't worry, I know how much you loved me." She had come back to comfort me. Sobbing myself awake, I finally felt an inner peace and happiness.

Aunt Ruth

CHAPTER 4

SPIRIT MANIFESTATIONS

Throughout the rest of this book you will find it very hard to believe how a typical average family who has always rejected the idea of there being such things as ghosts and spirits could turn into staunch believers. Although this next experience was quite trivial, it was the beginning of our initiation into the atmosphere of the spirit world.

One afternoon, three weeks after Ruth's funeral, I was in the kitchen making a sandwich for my youngest daughter, Mary Anne. I heard the utility room door open. Just like in a ghost movie, it sounded, "sque-e-e-e-ak," and stood ajar about eight inches. The utility room is located next to the kitchen, but one has to go down three steps to get to its level. It has two doors, both of which are interior and no windows. We keep one door locked; it goes into our bedroom. The other door has to be pushed back and forth with no way to lock it. The door is so heavy that it would take a very strong wind to open it. Knowing there was no way for this to happen I assumed there was a prowler in there. So I grabbed Mary Anne, then 6 years old, by the hand and ran over to my next-door neighbor Neva's house. She was one of my very best friends, much like a sister. We always lived next door to each other. She got her husband's gun, and we went back to catch the intruder. Well, needless to say, there was no one to apprehend. We thought that since my back door was unlocked that the prowler must have gone out that way. Satisfied after a thorough search of the premises that the burglar was gone, we went back to lunch and finished out the day in the usual manner.

When the rest of the family came home and heard of our experience, they thought it all to be very funny. Pete blamed the whole episode on a breeze. "How can you let a little breeze upset you so much," he smirked?

"Now, honey, where could a breeze possibly come from?" I replied. "Theres no way. Besides, the door had opened well as if someone had come out of the utility room."

But Pete is a scientist and is so-o-o-o technical. I thought maybe he was right. I wanted to believe him, anyway.

The very next afternoon while I was fixing supper, the same thing happened again. *Sque-e-e-e-ak*, again ajar about eight inches, and the door stood very still as though someone was in there and watching me. My spine tingled with fright as goose flesh crept over my body. We had lived in this house for five years, and until yesterday that door had never opened alone. Practically jerking Mary Anne out the front door, I stationed her on the last patio stone of our walkway by the curb and instructed her, "Don't take your eyes off the front door. If anyone comes out the house, you run as fast as you can over to Neva's. I'll keep my eye on you, so don't worry."

Racing Olympic style to my neighbors' house and beating on the door, I pleaded for her to hurry to get the gun, the prowler was back. I did not go into her house since I had to watch Mary Anne. As Neva and I flew back into the house, we told my daughter to stay outside. We did not want to go too close to the utility-room door, so as Neva pointed the gun at the door, I used a mop handle to push the door open. Standing there, trembling and demanding the invader to surrender, we saw nothing – no one was there. Searching the entire house and attic, we concluded that he must have gone out the back door again. Upon investigation we found the slide bolt still locked on the back door. If it wasn't a human being or a breeze, then what on Earth was it? Well, I left dinner unprepared, and Mary Anne and I sat outside until the family came home. I just could not stay in there alone. This time the group seemed sure that we were just concocting a story for the fun of it. Pete even acted a little disgusted with me; he thought I was making a mountain out of a mole hill.

On the third day in a row the phenomenon recurred, but this time the entire family was sitting at the supper table enjoying spareribs and swapping events of the day. The good old squeaky door did it again. *Sque-e-e-e-ak.*

Everyone present stopped eating; complete and utter silence swept the room. With eyes about to bulge out of their sockets, heads turned to see the noisy door that was standing open, staring in complete amazement. Pete whispered excitedly to us to "be quiet and keep on eating, just pretend you didn't hear anything, just don't move." He casually got up and walked to our bedroom to get his pistol.

I had to grin; Mary Anne chuckled out loud. "Let's see him get out of this without a nervous stomach," I thought. I watched very patiently as he lunged into the utility room ready to overpower the mysterious intruder. After a complete search of the entire house, he came back from the utility room as white as a sheet.

"Where is he, honey?" I giggled.

"There has to be a logical explanation, but that is scary as hell, isn't it?" he exclaimed. Later in the evening, after the girls were all asleep and tucked in to bed, we tried to reason out what had been transpiring in the past several days. Pete very apologetically took me into his arms and said, "Sorry I did not realize what you have been through. I can't understand unless a draft is coming in from somewhere. But don't worry, I'll work on a theory."

Next day I was in the kitchen preparing dinner when a spectacular idea hit me like a ton of bricks. I picked up the phone and called Neva. "Please come over. I have an experiment I want to try." Good old loyal, devoted friend Neva was there pronto.

"What do you have in mind," she inquired?

"Come with me; we're going to prove that it is the wind

opening the door." Taking my glass wind chimes from the living room we went in the pitch-dark utility room, turned on the light, and I proceeded to hang the chimes on a string directly in front of the door. "Okay," I said as I closed us up in the little room, "now would you agree that these are so placed that if a breeze or draft, strong enough to open that door passes by the chimes they would have to ring?"

"Most certainly" she agreed.

"We'll see. If I am in the kitchen and the door opens, I'll be very quiet and if I hear the chimes then we'll have proven a point, right?" As we stood there reassuring each other, all these words fresh out of our mouths, the door opened wide with its *sque-e-e-e-ak*. Our eyes went immediately to the very still chimes. They never moved, tingled or anything.

"Oh, my God," Neva screamed.

We both yelled hysterically as we darted through the open door, each trying to outrun the other. We fell up the steps. I skinned my knees, and my foot scraped the back of her heel as we scampered out the front door. The only thing we managed to prove was that this was not a human being or a natural phenomenon. The only possible conclusion was that it was a supernatural power, an experience of the unknown. Needless to say, I remained in a chair on our front lawn until Pete came home. Nothing could have made me stay in that house.

After a very serious family conference, we decided it had to be a spirit, but who? Or what? The only recent deceased person we could think of was Aunt Ruth. Then I remembered a week before she died, I had been talking to her on the telephone. She was really depressed, wondering what would become of her when she got really old. Now she had a good son and I knew he would take care of her, but she was feeling sorry for herself. I said to her, "Ruth, don't ever worry about being alone because I love you and if need be, you could always come live with me."

"That's the nicest thing anybody ever said to me," she tearfully replied.

"Lord, maybe she took me up on my proposal. Honey, do you suppose?"

"Perhaps, but we can't be sure," Pete said. If it was her she would never hurt us, I reasoned. She would only be there because she loved us.

Being completely honest, I have never been so scared in my entire life. Goose pimples became my natural daily attire. The children were afraid to go to sleep, and we started leaving all the lights on at night. I was petrified to go into the kitchen alone, and I never went into the utility room to wash clothes without my husband. My nerves were almost to the breaking point. Who would ever believe we have a spirit living in our home? I could hardly go that route myself.

After several months had passed things had quieted down somewhat. I was washing dishes and I was alone in the house. Ruth made her presence known by way of the squeaky door. Now I had to confront her. I rinsed off my hands and turned around facing an empty kitchen. "All right, Ruth," I said out loud, "I know you are here and you are more than welcome to live with us, but you will have to be quiet and don't make so much noise because you are scaring us to death. We all love you, but please go about the house silently." Then I went on with my work, feeling rather stupid but glad no one had heard me (maybe only Ruth). I feel she must have understood because suddenly the door closed. It was at this point that we were able to accept the housing of her spirit and her constant presence. We learned eventually to laugh and joke about her and we know she was happy living with us. When something would go wrong and no one would 'fess up to doing it, somebody would say it was probably Auth Ruth. I know Ruth would have been laughing right along with all of us.

Of course, many of these weird occurrences had been told or witnessed by our daughters and many young friends. They thought it was simply great having a haunted house around the neighborhood. Young people today seem to enjoy the mystery surrounding the unknown, extra sensory perception, flying saucers, the occult, palmistry, and the Ouija Board.

Stew, a great friend, but more like a son, dropped by one day to say hello. He had brought another young man to meet us. The new friend was a full-blooded Cherokee Indian and a professional Indian dancer. He was presently employed as a private in the U.S. Army. The three of us sat in the living room discussing Indian dances, when as plain as day we could hear someone walk down the hall from the bedroom wing, coming through the living room within five feet of us. The footsteps stopped at the entrance to the dining room, then came back and retraced the same path.

"What was that," whispered the Indian.

"Aunt Ruth, I guess," trembled Stew.

Their visit ended very abruptly. "Bye now, come back soon," I called after them.

"Yes, ma'am," he stuttered, "but I really remember something I had to do this afternoon." He never returned.

Another afternoon, October 26, 1969 at 2 p.m., when Stew was visiting for dinner, we were in my kitchen. I was preparing some potatoes and he was writing a letter to his mom. I was singing some little song to myself, when all of a sudden the back door burst open and little Mary Anne dashed through the room on the way to wash here hands in the bathroom. She had been making mud-pies in the yard. We could hear her splashing the water and bumping the soap dish. Then we heard the sweetest humming.

"Isn't that adorable," Stew remarked, looking up from his letter. "I didn't know she had such a beautiful voice; she sounds like a little angel."

At that moment I stepped to the bathroom door, looked at my sweet girl and said, "That's pretty, honey."

"What?" She questioned.

"Your humming," I replied.

"That wasn't me, I haven't said a word," she said as she hurried past me to go back outside.

As I shrugged my shoulders in disbelief and returned to my potato peeling, the humming became audible once again. Stew's eyes flashed quickly to meet mine. "Ruth?," he asked me.

I shivered! Out loud I pleaded, "All right, Ruth, you can stay, but you must be quiet; you're scaring us, but we are glad you are happy." At that very second the humming ceased.

Madeline, our sixteen-year-old daughter, asked her daddy one evening to change a light bulb in her ceiling fixture because it had burned out. Securing a ladder, Pete climbed up and just as he reached out to touch the bulb, it came back on again. Thinking that the bulb was loose, he tried to screw it in a bit tighter, but to no avail, for it was tight as a drum already. Down the ladder he came. Off went the light. Up he went, on went the light. Down, off, up, on.

"It must be a loose wire, girls, leave the light switch off tonight," he instructed.

Next morning we called an electrician to check the wires. He found nothing wrong.

"Well, why does the light blink," I asked.

"Have no idea but its nothing I can find. Everything seems to be perfect," he concluded. It was Ruth playing games, we guessed. Madeline wouldn't sleep in there alone after that. She slept with Kathleen.

One afternoon I drove my mother to her sister Lovie's house to deliver some artificial flowers we had bought for her. While we were there Lovie made the statement that Ruth was about to drive her out of her mind. Shocked to hear her speak of Ruth's presence, I pursued it further. "What are you talking about," I asked.

"You would never believe me if I told you that Ruth opens and closes my closet door all the time. You remember that I brought some of her clothes home to wear?" I nodded. "Well, all of her things are in that closet. I am going to give them all away if she will just leave me alone," she remarked.

"Now, Lovie, let me tell you something that you won't believe either." I then related to her all the encounters we had

had. "Just remember one thing," I concluded, "Ruth loved us very much and if she has come back it is only because she wants to be with us. That is why is trying so-o-o-o desperately to let us know that she is here. She knows that you and I would be the most likely candidates to understand what all this means because we are closest to her. Our relationship being almost that of a mother-daughter and yours being a very companionable sister relationship. Besides, who else in the family could she go to that would believe in spirits? Just talk to her and be happy that you two can still be together." Even today (several years later) Lovie's closet door still does its thing! But it no longer makes her nervous.

My father-in-law, who was widowed, lived alone in his big house until he became ill. He then moved into the house with his sister, who also lived alone, until he could regain his strength. To help him out we would go over to the old homestead everyday and check around, being sure all the doors and windows were secure. We turned on night lights each night to discourage prowlers. The house was very far back off the road and sat on the middle of an acre of land. It was extremely quiet there. So from time to time, when I wanted to be alone for a moment of peace and quiet, I would take a sandwich and sit quietly in the sunroom. It was great to be away from all the neighborhood noise. Not one sound to be heard except the birds singing and the squirrels chattering.

One chilly October afternoon about lunch time, I hurried there to relax and write a couple of letters. I went into the sunroom and was accomplishing my project, when suddenly I heard, most distinctly, ice cubes being dropped into a glass. The noise came from the kitchen. I was petrified and thought, "Oh my God, somebody is in the house with me." Then I heard another ice cube being dropped into the glass. I had to pass the kitchen in order to get out of the house. I quietly picked up my keys and, peeping around the sunroom door, I saw no one in the kitchen. As panic swept over my entire body, I raced out the door and to my car.

Outside I saw a neighbor watering his garden. I hollered to him to please come over. Hurrying to greet him, I explained what had happened. He picked up a hoe for protection and we went back into the house together to make a search. We found no one, no glass, no ice. After dinner that evening, I told Pete of the incident. I said it sounded like someone was making himself a drink. Then Pete reminded me that every day while his mother was living, she would go into the kitchen just before lunch and make cocktails for his dad and for herself. Well, no one could ever convince me that I had not heard three ice cubes being dropped into a glass. There is no other sound to equal it.

The next day I had to do my daily check of the place, but to avoid that "alone feeling" and also have something living along for company, I took our big German shepherd dog, Buffy, with me. Buffy was quite an aggressive dog and did not like strangers, so I felt safe. We drove up and Buffy, wagging her tail happily, could hardly wait to get out of the car. She loved to come over and would always run up to the front door and wait for us to open it. Then she would dash through the living room into the kitchen, and when I would open the back door she would run and race in the back yard, chasing squirrels and having a magnificent time. However, this day we drove up in the yard and she barked happily for me to hurry and get out. Running up on the porch as usual, she sat impatiently as I fumbled for the key. Finally I flung open the door and Buffy took two steps inside and stood perfectly still. It appeared that she was watching something move around the room. Her eyes staring at nothing I could see, she started growling and backing out the front door. And Buffy backs down to *nobody*. So what in the world was wrong with her?

I got her by the collar, patted her and told her it was all right, but she still refused to come in any farther. So I tried dragging her. She whined, pulled away from me and darted back to the car. Needless to say, so did I! What she saw or felt I will never know. But nobody could never know the feeling that swept over me, either. I never went back there alone.

One Sunday morning, bright and early, my three daughters and I were getting ready for church. I noticed Pete was still in his pajamas and robe. "Aren't you going to church with us?" I asked.

"No, I really do not feel good. I have a sore throat. I thought I would just stay home and rest," he replied.

"Shame, shame, shame on Daddy," laughed our girls, as we filed out the door and into the car. "Just kidding," they hollered out of the car windows as we drove off.

After Mass we returned home only to find Pete very upset. He was sitting in a big chair by the front door. He was holding Maggie, our little fox terrier, in his arms. We seldom allowed her in the house and never on the furniture. Upon observing this very unusual scene we quickly asked, "What is going on?"

Pete answered, "Well I was sitting in this chair reading and I kept feeling a presence, like someone was in the room with me. So I let Maggie in so I wouldn't be alone."

As I went back to my reading Maggie started growling and looking around the living room toward the ceiling. She appeared to be watching something moving around the room. Suddenly she started shaking as if she was terrified. Then she yelped and jumped in my lap, climbed up to my shoulder, turning her head so that her eyes were shielded by my neck. The adrenaline suddenly surging through my body was enough confirmation to assure me we were not alone. Then I felt a pocketful of real cool air cross the room.

"Scary as hell," Pete stuttered.

"Just Ruth keeping you company," I said.

"You should have gone with us to church," the girls all giggled.

"I don't think that this is very funny," he exclaimed, "but I do think I'd be feeling better now if I had gone to church."

CHAPTER 5

NEVA'S UNNERVING EXPERIENCES

Writing about Ruth's belongings reminds me that when Ruth was alive, she would upon occasion give some of her old clothes to me. She would say, "Now if they don't fit you, give them to Neva." Ruth thought it was funny that we were so happy to get hand-me-downs. After she had passed away and Irvin had given me so many of her personal articles, there happened to be some of the underwear, sweaters, etc., that were a little large for me, so naturally I gave them to Neva.

The next day my telephone rang. "Mildred, come quick, you'll never believe what is happening over here." I scurried across the lawn and jumped the hedges between our houses. Neva looked like a wreck as she greeted me. "I'm here all alone in the house, so I want you to see something." Curiously I followed her to the dining room. "Nobody would ever take my word for something like this," she said. She had washed all the underwear she had inherited (so to speak) from Ruth in the same wash load with the rest of her family's laundry. Later, after the wash had dried, she began folding the clothes and sorting them on the dining room table. All was fine until she picked up a piece of Ruth's belongings. Immediately a loud knock came from the wall near the table.

As I stood there aghast, I observed her pick up a child's sock, then her child's shorts . . . nothing happened. But as soon as she would pick up any of Ruth's apparel: *knock . . . knock.* This continued through the entire laundry load. It gave us gooseflesh.

Neva said, "Do you think she wants them back?"

"No," I told her. "I think she just wants to tell you to enjoy them."

Like me, Neva was a very superstitious person. When her father died, she kept a pair of his old shoes and put them in her bedroom closet. She would often tell me that as she lay in bed at night, she could hear his shoes walking and moving around. I suggested that she take a piece of white chalk and trace around each shoe. Then when she heard the sounds again she could look and see if the shoes had moved. *"Heavens, no,"* she shrieked. "If they had moved I'd have a heart attack. Besides, as the old saying goes, 'ignorance is bliss.'"

One morning after that conversation, Neva had gotten her husband off to work and had taken the children to school. She was gone no longer than five minutes. When she returned home she came to my house and asked if I had seen her husband come back to the house after she left.

"Nope, I sure didn't, why?" I asked.

"Well, I left the house locked and nothing has been disturbed and the front door is still locked, but I want you to look."

As we entered her front door, she pointed at the living-room rug. There were very large, muddy footprints on the carpet. The prints went across the living room and down the hall, turning toward her bedroom closet. There they stopped abruptly. She was petrified.

"Now come in here, I want to show you something else weird." Her family always ate their meals at the dining-room table. After her husband had gone to work this particular morning she had cleaned off the table, put a fresh tablecloth on it and replaced the centerpiece. But on this "fresh" tablecloth was a segment of what appeared to be cigarette ashes still clustered together as though someone had nonchalantly tapped a cigarette to remove the ash.

I suggested that she call her husband at work, assuring her that it had to be his footprints and ashes. She immediately phoned him. He informed her that he had *not* gone back into the house. She was shaking nervously as she explained to me that she had seen her deceased father several times in the past week standing in her yard by her clothes line, and he was the only one she knew that allowed ashes to build up on the end of a cigarette and tap them off for his own amusement. (You can believe this or not, but I'll swear its the truth. We both felt that we knew the answer to the mystery.)

There were lots of times that Neva and I would go to neighborhood parties for new brides or to baby showers for expectant mothers. Usually at least one person at the party knew of our scary, stirring experiences. Invariably, the subject of spooks and spirits would come up for general discussion. Then it always turned out the same way. Neva and I would tell of all our spine-chilling adventures, leaving everybody else there scared to death. We would even have to walk the different women to their automobiles when it was time to go home because they were afraid that ghosts would be after them. We would laugh and laugh and laugh. I sometimes think they did not believe us; perhaps thought that we were making up all the stories. Nevertheless, we were always the hit of all gatherings.

In May of 1975, I had another night vision. I saw a very large box. As I approached it and looked inside, I found three skeletons, This greatly disturbed me! Within three weeks there were three deaths of close friends. First to go was a neighbor, then Neva's husband died. She had been very sick herself, having had cancer for a period of time and several operations. Several weeks after she had been widowed, she too passed into the world of the spirits. I still feel very close to her; she was like a sister to me. As I write this book, I relive the companionship we shared. I feel like she is standing behind me as I type about our escapades. I find myself sitting here alone during the wee hours typing and laughing at us, or reminiscing but not dwelling on the more solemn events.

For years, Neva and I would visit her sister at Isle of Hope. On the way we had to pass an old house sitting high upon a hill overlooking the marsh and river. The house had a large front porch and with two very large rocking chairs. Neva and I would joke about the chairs.

"I'd love to sit up there and rock all day," Neva said.

"Me too," I replied.

"Tell you what, when we get real old and don't have anything to do we can buy this old house together and rock all day and all night," said Neva.

"Great," I replied.

Every time for about the next five years we would laugh as we rode past that house, and we would say in unison, "There's our rocking chairs."

Would you believe the day after Neva passed into the other world, I was riding to her sister's house to take food for her family, and when I came to the old house, I glanced up at *our porch*. Much to my astonishment and grief, one of the rocking chairs was gone. Only "mine" remained. Totally grieved over her chair being gone, it was years before I could ever go down that road again.

Neva, my friend, I love you and miss you.

CHAPTER 6

VISIONS OF STRANGE HAPPENINGS

On a very dark, dreary, misty July 17, 1973, I had gone to church to attend a funeral service for a friend. Later, driving in the procession to the cemetery for the burial, the raindrops started to lightly sprinkle my windshield. So I decided to make a quick turn out of the line of cars so I could dash home and get my umbrella and catch up with the others at the next intersection. Upon arriving at home I hurriedly opened the front door and noticed immediately that the whole house was aglow with a yellowish light. *Mercy me, who in the world left on all these lights?* I thought. Every light in the house was on. *Oh, well.* I ran to the closet to procure the umbrella and then to the lamps to turn them off. I was totally dumbfounded to discover that *not one* lamp was turned on, and yet on this dismal sunless day, my home was aglow in a beautiful yellow light. Reflection? No way. Needless to say, I hightailed out of there *pronto. . .*

I only wish I had, at that time, been able to understand all that I know now, because I believe that beautiful glow was something good, warm and Godly. But I was too afraid to allow myself to enjoy the beauty or investigate it. Perhaps if I had been more mature I would have asked if the Lord were there. For only one other time did I witness such a beautiful glow. I will come to that part shortly.

Not too long ago while doing some research on these matters, I came across a psychic who had had a similar experience, and I was excited to have a better understanding of this occurrence.

I had not had any visions in almost a year; I was too afraid after having seen Ruth's death. One night I was sitting straight up in bed and I could hardly keep my eyes open.

"Why don't you lie down and go to sleep?" Pete asked.

"No, because I might have a vision and see something bad. Why don't I ever see something good?"

"You probably do, but you don't pay attention to the good things. I'll tell you what," he insisted, "try to relax and the next time you see something, no matter how silly or trivial it is, tell me about it and we will see if we can find a meaning."

"Okay, I will," I yawned. Building up my courage I snuggled cozily in the covers, closed my eyes and started to drift off. Suddenly I bolted up in bed, laughing my head off. "Okay, you want to share this unmeaning vision with me. This is so silly I am sure it means nothing."

"Let's have it." Pete waited anxiously.

"Well-l-l, I saw an ancient tomb with hieroglyphics on the wall, and inside the tomb was a piece of paper blowing gently as though in a breeze. Then it came closer. I tried to read what was on the paper but it appeared to be real hazy except for the numbers 4X. That's all I could read. Now you simply can't make anything out of that,"I chuckled.

"Maybe something is going to happen four times," he reasoned.

"Don't be silly," I replied as I tried to go back to sleep.

The next morning was the one-year anniversary of Ruth's death. As I busied myself preparing breakfast, Madeline, my sixteen-year-old, was reading different articles to me from the morning newspaper. "Guess what, Mother? Irvin (Ruth's son) has a memorial article in here about Aunt Ruth."

"That's real nice, honey, read it to me."

After she finished she exclaimed, "Mother, somebody else put a memorial in here too about Aunt Ruth. It said *By her Mother, Father, Sisters and Brothers*."

"How odd," I stammered. Then her sweet voice shrieked even higher, stuttering "Mother, the same articles are in here again. That makes four times."

IN LOVING MEMORY OF
MRS. RUTH B. STALL
Who died one year ago,
March 3, 1966
The depths of sorrow we cannot tell,
Of the loss of one we loved so well,
And while she sleeps a peaceful sleep,
Her memory we shall always keep.
Sadly missed by
SON, DAUGHTER-IN-LAW,
GRANDCHILDREN

IN MEMORIAM
MRS. RUTH B. STALL
Who passed away one year ago,
March 3, 1966
Sometimes it is hard why some thing
have to be,
But in his wisdom, God had planned
beyond our power to see,
In our hearts there is a picture more
precious than silver or gold,
It's a picture of our dear one, whose
memory will never grow old.
Days of sorrow still come over us, al-
though you left us one year ago.
We miss that smile and ever will, your
absence here no one can fill,
We mourn down here but not in vain,
For in heaven we hope to see your
smiling face again.
You are not forgotten, Ruth,
Nor will you ever be, as long as life
and memory last.
Loves Greatest Gift-Remembrance.
Sadly missed by
FATHER, MOTHER,
SISTERS and BROTHERS

IN MEMORIAM
In Loving Memory of
MRS. RUTH B. STALL
Who died 1 year ago, March 3, 1966
The depths of sorrow we cannot tell,
Of the loss of one we loved so well,
And while she sleeps a peaceful sleep,
Her memory we shall always keep.
Sadly missed by
SON, DAUGHTER-IN-LAW,
GRANDCHILDREN

IN MEMORIAM
In loving memory of our dear one
MRS. RUTH B. STALL
Who passed away one year ago,
March 3, 1966
Sometimes it is hard why somethings
have to be,
But in his wisdom, God had planned
beyond our power to see,
In our hearts there is a picture more
precious than silver or gold,
It's a picture of our dear one, whose
memory will never grow old.
Days of sorrow still come over us, al-
though you left us 1 year ago.
We miss that smile and ever will,
your absence here no one can fill,
We mourn down here but not in vain,
for in heaven we hope to see your
smiling face again.
You are not forgotten, Ruth, nor will
you ever be, as long as life and
memory last.
Loves Greatest Gift—Remembrance
Sadly missed by
FATHER, MOTHER,
SISTERS AND BROTHERS

The newspaper had printed the four identical articles straight in a row. Pete hurried to the kitchen to see about all the excitement and was quite thrilled when he realized that in my vision the tomb had been a symbol or death and the hieroglyphics had meant news about the dead. Then of course, the 4X meant I would hear about death four times, which is exactly what was in the newspaper. Wonders never cease.

When spring came we decided to hop in the car and go to Florida to see my sister, Ann, and her family for a much-needed vacation. We had a glorious time just chewing the fat and resting our weary bones. The three days went by much too fast. After all the *adieus*, we headed north on U.S. 17. Driving along quietly about 4 p.m., I glanced through the windshield and saw a huge fire in the distance in the middle of the road.

"What in the world is on fire up there?" I worried.

"I don't see any fire," Pete said.

"Straight ahead, honey, look at it billowing."

"Sorry, Babe, you're seeing things again, there is no fire," he insisted. As we rode on, I apologized to everyone because I had been so silly. There was no sign of a fire anywhere.

When we arrived back in Savannah, we stopped by my mother's house before going home. She rushed out to the car and questioned, "Did you have a vision while you were gone?" "No, why?" I replied.

"Well, at four o'clock this afternoon Uncle Charlie's house burned to the ground!"

"Oh, Babe, I am sorry. I shouldn't have made fun," Pete apologized. "I should have realized."

A few days later, very tired and having worked in the yard all day, I plopped down on the sofa to take a break. Closing my eyes to rest for a minute, I saw Pete's good friend, Jim, holding his head as though in pain. At this same moment I began experiencing heaviness in my chest. I sat up quickly and realized that the pain wasn't mine but Jim's. When Pete came in from the yard, I asked if he had seen Jim lately, and he said that Jim had gone to North Carolina on vacation. I told Pete about it and he shrugged it off. Three days later we heard that Jim had suffered from ptomaine poisoning and had become so sick that he suffered a heart attack and died.

When the children came home from school next afternoon I was sitting at the kitchen table drawing a picture. When they inquired about my doodling, I explained that I was drawing something I had seen. The image was a very swampy area with numerous tall, old cedar trees. There were lots of lily pads floating in the swampy algae-laden water at the base of the trees.

The children and I could not associate this specific scene with any location locally. But several days later Pete's Uncle Raymond died, and he was buried in Bluffton, S.C. The family, en route to the funeral, had just crossed the Savannah River when we came to the Wildlife Refuge. The children were the first to recognize the scene. At the top of their voices they screamed, "There it is, there it is! Exactly!"

Mary Anne went to a little neighborhood store with Pete to buy some Cokes and snacks for the usual crowd of teenagers that came over to visit every Saturday evening. Vacuuming the carpet, I suddenly felt a wave of panic come over me. I yelled to Kathleen and Madeline, "Get the car keys and come quick. Something has happened to Mary Anne." We were going to hurry around the corner to find out what was wrong. As we approached my car, Pete and Mary Anne rode up. "Thank the Lord." I said as I laughingly walked to their car and feeling kind of foolish for my previous behavior. "I'm glad you are here. While you were gone I felt something terrible had happened to Mary Anne. Isn't that silly?"

Pete said, "Look," as he uncovered her little leg. It was gaped and bleeding. "Hop in, we have to take her to the hospital to get some stitches." He then related that as she was standing near some large Pepsi bottles, one exploded and cut her on the leg. We could feel our mouths drop in awe.

Kathleen had gone to Augusta, Georgia, for a golf tournament with a friend. About an hour before she was due back home, I envisioned the car she was in, stooped in the middle of the road but I could only see the bottom part of the car, below the level of the windows. I could see Kathleen in her stocking feet and the skirt part of her black-and-white polka-dot dress. She was running in front of the car as though they were changing drivers' seats. I was a little uneasy but not upset. When they arrived home, I asked if they had stopped in the middle of the road. They said they had decided to return home on the back highway instead of the Interstate because the fall leaves were so beautiful. A deer had run across the road and almost hit the car. Kathleen had been driving and the incident had shaken her so badly that she didn't want to drive any more. So she had opened her door and had run in front of the car to get into the passenger side.

One morning I was almost awake when a spirit, Florrie, Pete's mother, appeared to me. She said, "Give the Madonna (a vase) to Kathleen, the Silver Silent Butler to Madeline, and the two blue-and-white vases to Mary Anne." You might say that I was "spooked awake." I jumped out of bed, astounded. I could not believe hearing from her in such a manner. Still in my nightgown, I hurriedly gathered up everything she had named so I wouldn't forget.

I awakened Pete with the news, "Hey, your mom was here," and explained what had transpired. I was wondering why these particular articles were assigned to the respective children. When the other girls and Mary Anne woke up I presented them with their gifts from Grandma Florrie. Then we realized that Kathleen had always loved the Madonna Vase and would pick flowers, and weeds, and bring them to her for the Madonna. Madeline was the only one that smoked, so she needed the Silent Butler. I had never noticed that the blue-and-white vases had horses on them. Mary Anne had a big white horse (Sam).

Struggling to get to sleep one night, I had a quick picture come into my mind's eye. A man appeared in front of me wearing a big pair of dark sunshades. *That's crazy, its cold outside! How strange.*

Next morning Madeline was busy pushing the dust mop around her bedroom floor. She leaned the handle against the bedpost while she picked up something off the rug. When she raised up she accidentally hit the mop and the top of the handle hit her in the eye. She was in such pain that I took her to the optometrist, and when we walked into his office . . . there in a corner was the old man sitting there wearing a pair of dark sunshades. Incidentally, Madeline had a scratch on her eyeball so she came out with a patch on her eye.

I know all of this is hard to believe but every single word in this book is true!

My grandmother was in the hospital and I had planned to take my mother to see her the next morning, Meanwhile, the night before I had a preview of the coming events. My mind's eye saw a corner with three ladies standing and talking. One lady left and another woman, wearing a hat, came up. One of the ladies fell on the floor. That was all I saw.

Next morning, Mother and I went to the hospital and as we walked down the hall my cousin, Maree, came up to us, so we stopped to chat as Mother walked on to Grandmother's room. As we stood there, a lady walked up and asked if we could direct her to a telephone as she had to call her home. We pointed to a telephone a few steps away. Thanking us, she went toward the phone and at that moment, a nurse wearing a white cap came up to Maree and asked if we knew where the lady had gone. We told the nurse, "She is using the telephone." The nurse waited near us, and when the lady finished her short conversation, the nurse approached her and told her that her husband had just passed away. The lady fainted at our feet. All this occurred where two halls crossed and we were standing against the wall . . . right at a corner.

It is hard to believe such a series of events is predestined. If we had not arrived at that exact moment, I would have missed Maree, and if the lady had not decided at that exact moment to call home, and if her husband had not died at that exact moment, the nurse would not have looked for the woman. And if she had not been told about her husband's death at that corner by a nurse wearing a cap, next to Maree and me, she wouldn't have collapsed at our feet.

CHAPTER 7

GRANDCHILDREN SIGHTINGS

I mentioned the fact that all three of my granddaughters have the *Cross La Mystic* on their hands. This assures me that all three will have some form of psychic ability. To what degree or in which manner I do not know at this time, for their ages are presently 5, 6 and 7 years old. The lines are there but the mounts are not fully developed yet. I have already begun at their tender ages to introduce them casually to the major lines, namely the head, heart, life, fate and the family ring. While they are young they can learn about the mounts and different happy markings. If I live long enough to watch them become young ladies, and if they are particularly interested, then I will consider several things before I decide if I will, or will not, disclose to one, or all of them, the secrets that I have discovered.

A person has to be emotionally strong and mature enough to handle unhappy events that sometimes unfold before their eyes. They also have to be wise enough and have the good judgment to know what to tell and what to hold back. Their words will have to reap encouragement to their subjects. I will have to be sure that they only want to read palms because they feel its a gift and a privilege from the Lord. They would have to reassure me they will only use it for some good to honor Him. For He is the bearer of their gift.

My three granddaughters, Suzie, Chrissy, and Rebecca each have already had several psychic experiences. I seriously doubt that when they are older that they will remember these incidents, so I want to jot them down for the record.

One evening, shortly after my father-in-law died, the family was relaxing in our living room. Suzie, three years old at the time, was playing on the floor by herself. She went underneath an old antique table that had belonged to her great-grandfather and was sitting there quietly with her doll. Suddenly she screamed and crawled from under the table as fast as she could. She jumped into her mother's lap, hysterical.

"What's wrong, baby?" Madeline asked.

"That man under the table scared me," she cried.

"What man?" Madeline questioned.

She pointed to *nothing* under the table and said, "There, see him?" Cold flesh came over all of us. Suddenly the living room became vacant. Everybody decided to go home.

An afternoon shortly after that, Suzie and Chrissy (then 2 years old) were in the playroom in our house. Suzie was busy putting lots of toys in the crib for Chrissy. Chrissy was standing in the crib laughing at Suzie when suddenly Suzie screamed and ran out of the room. "Mama, Mama, there's a man in there." Madeline and I and ran to see. When we got to the room, of course, no one was there that we could see. But Chrissy was standing up and waving at a corner of the ceiling and laughing. Suzie fearfully pointed up to the same corner and whispered, "See him, Mama?"

We took both of the children outside for the rest of the afternoon.

A year later my father had passed away. Sitting quietly at the lunch table, Suzie, with a big mouthful of peanut butter and jelly, looked first at the ceiling and then at me and calling me by my nickname, said, "Pooh, your daddy wants me to tell you that he loves you and misses you very much." I almost fell out of my chair. Then she smiled and announced, "And you know what else he said? That he loves me and Chrissy too."

Almost choking on my cracker, I asked, "How do you know that?"

"I could hear him, silly Pooh, don't you hear people when they talk to you?" I know in my heart she heard my father, because she was too young to concoct such a story.

About sixty years ago there was a children's home that took in abused, abandoned and unwanted babies and small children. After years of wonderful service to the community, the cottage was turned into a home for older troubled boys.

A very good friend of ours worked there for awhile. Lots of repairs were needed so they cleaned out the attic and sold various articles that had been discarded. They also sold several very old, high-back wooden rocking chairs. The chairs were beautiful; one could see the paint worn off where the women had sat for many years, rocking the babies. Even where their heads had rested against the back of the chair was worn. Kathleen was fortunate to have acquired one. She had put the chair in the bedroom of her little girl, Rebecca. One night, Rebecca, then two years old, was playing in her room, when suddenly she started screaming and crying in a hysterical outburst. Running to see what was wrong, Kathleen picked her up to comfort her. The child was terrified!

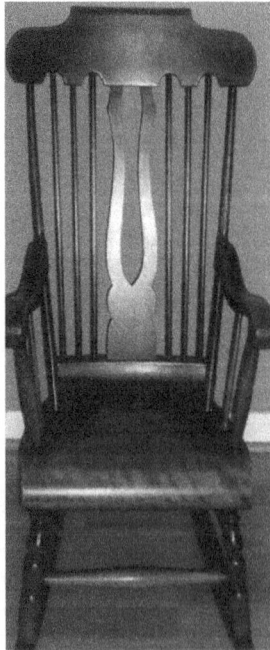

Kathleen thought maybe a bug of some sort had been in the room. "Baby, Baby its all right . . . what 's the matter?" she asked.

Rebecca, clinging to her mother desperately, pointed to the rocking chair in the corner and said, "There's a lady in that chair." She was quickly reassured that no one was there, but she would not let Kathleen put her down. "Yes, yes!" Rebecca screamed. "See the lady?"

They went into the den and called me on the telephone, asking "What can we do?" I instructed her to remove the chair and put it in the living room right away . . . and to let Rebecca sleep with her that night so she would feel secure. I feel a spirit from the past was attached to that chair and had rocked many babies in it.

Therefore, she was happy when the chair was put in a little child's room. She wouldn't have hurt Rebecca, but she could scare her. I told them to leave the chair in the other room. It was a very long time before the child would go in her bedroom alone.

It is an accepted belief that young children are more receptive than adults when it comes to seeing apparitions. It is because their little innocent minds are not clouded up with problems of the world; this makes them more susceptible.

An unexplained phenomenon occurred with our year-old grandson, Michael. His vocabulary was made up of only three words: Ma-ma, Da-da and bye-bye . . . that was all. One afternoon I was holding him in my arms. I walked over to the kitchen sink to watch Pete cleaning a fish. As the baby and I stood slightly behind Pete, Michael put his tiny little hand on his granddad's shoulder and patting him sweetly, said out loud, "I love you."

Shocked, Pete turned around and said, "Well, I love you too!"

How could this have happened? Could this be a hint of reincarnation here?

Mary Anne and I were standing in our living room one afternoon when we saw a black shadow-like figure walk out of the utility room and down the hall. It disappeared as quickly as it had appeared. We were so shaken back by this, we clutched each other tightly and began to shiver. The next afternoon we had word that our grandfather had died.

Kathleen called me from work, "Mother, has Mary Anne come hone from school yet?"

"Sure," I said.

"Well, don't let her go outside today because as I lay in bed this morning I saw a snake bite her." We laughed! About 5 p.m. I sent Mary Anne out to take some trash to the garbage can. The dog started barking and Mary Anne started screaming. I ran out to see a snake curled up by the garbage can. Then she and I and the dog ran into the house. I don't know what happened to the snake!

Once Kathleen dreamed that she was at a funeral but did not know the corpse in the casket. As she was backing away from it, she realized that her friends, Alvin and Dora, were there. When she saw them later the next day, she was telling them about her dream and they told her that Alvin's grandfather had died that night.

My granddaughters, now 15 and 16 years old, requested that I put some of their strange happenings in this book.

"OPENING MY MOUTH" . . . By Rebecca

September 24, 1994 at 8 p.m., I was at the airport to pick up my ten year old stepbrother, Keith. He was coming from Wyoming to live with us. Mom and I were standing in front of a big glass window watching the Delta flight pull into view. We were all excited, waiting for the plane to land. As the passengers began to exit, and we were anxiously waiting for him, I said, jokingly, "I have an awful thought. Wouldn't it be terrible if he wasn't on the plane?"

Mom replied, "Don't say a thing like that!"

However, much to our shock and dismay everyone got off the plane except three people, Keith, another little boy and a woman whose fiancée was there, waiting. They had had a six-hour delay due to engine trouble, so most of the passengers transferred to another plane that had a few seats available.

Those few were able to continue their journey on to Savannah. It was distressingly unthinkable that they would bump the children, but they did. And their parents were not notified. I cannot tell you how furious the parents were. They had to go to the ticket office to find out if the children were safe and would be on the 2 a.m. plane.

A week or so later, Thomas, my step-dad, was taking me to school. "As we passed a local Catholic hospital, I said very seriously, I bet that hospital will eventually merge with the other Catholic hospital across town."

"No, they are both too independent; it won't happen," he replied.

The next day, going to school, we heard on the radio that a meeting was scheduled that day for the two hospitals to discuss a merger. Thomas said, "You said that yesterday!"

"I know," I answered.

CHAPTER 8

UNEXPLAINED PHENOMENA

Several days later as I pulled up to the traffic light in my car, I had the feeling that something was wrong at home. So I stepped on the gas, and when I got home I ran around to the back yard. I felt as though I was going to see my husband hurt and lying on the ground. When I did not see him, I ran into the house where he was talking with his aunt on the telephone. Relieved, I plopped down in a chair to listen to his conversation, only to discover that he was upset. His aunt had called to let him know that his seventy-five-year-old father had fallen on the ground and hurt himself a few minutes before I got home. I do wish people would get off my brain-waves. It keeps me a nervous wreck!

Taking Mary Anne to the Kiddie Fair, I had a weird feeling that a specific man standing alone in a dimly lit area was going to approach her. I quickly took her by the hand and told her, "Stay by me as I am sure that man is watching you." Out of the corner of my eye I saw him advance toward her. I turned toward him, he smiled and held out five tickets for rides.

He said, "You are such a cute little girl, ask your mother if you can have these tickets, I don't need them." Relieved, I smiled back and thanked him, but still continued holding her hand firmly.

My mind's eye saw my own father wiping tears from his eyes, then holding his head. I went to the phone to call and check on him, only to find out that he was upset because his brother, John, had died.

I was laughing so hard one morning that Pete inquired what

was so funny. I related that just before I had opened my eyes, I had seen a man lying in a bed, sleeping with a wool stocking hat on his head. But this was not so funny after all. We found that a cousin of Pete's, who was very old and who lived alone, had been dead for five days. They found him lying in bed. Evidently the hat represented the fact that he was *cold*.

At a kindergarten where I worked, it was about time for the Health Department to send an Inspector out to check our building. So I informed the Church Secretary to watch out for him as the kindergarten had scheduled a field trip. I told her, "You will know him because he has only one arm and his name is Mr. Perry." Wanda, the other teacher, argued that that wasn't his name and that the man that had come last time had both arms. It was a friendly disagreement, so we left it in the confused state and took the children on the trip. When we returned the secretary was very nervous. She told us the inspector had come. His name was Mr. Perry and he did have only one arm, but he told her he had *never* been to our school until that day! *Strange!* How can that be explained?

One Sunday afternoon, Madeline and a few of our young friends, Ken, Stew, and my nephew, Leon III, all wanted to go to the Jacksonville Zoo. Pete and I didn't have enough room in our car, so they asked Kathleen if they could borrow her old, black, raggedy car she had purchased from my father when she started working. She said, "Yes, but only if Leon III drives." All agreed.

The night before we left I had a vision. I saw the back of Kathleen's car shimmering pretty bad, and as I watched it, three black disk-like objects flew from it. That was all but it unnerved me.

`The next morning I cautioned Leon III to drive very carefully as I explained what I had seen. I told him we would follow them. "Now, if you have any trouble, stop, and we will help you," I said. I was afraid that three bad things would happen. Everybody piling in we started out. Halfway to Brunswick they had a blow-out on the left rear tire. We all stopped and the boys changed it. Well that was number one.

When we were at the zoo, we all had so much fun. Stew wielding a big stick he found, hopped onto a bench in the park and pretended to be sword fighting with an invisible swordsman. Suddenly he fell and landed, sitting on the ground. As he got back up on his feet he announced, "Hey, you guys, that felt like someone pushed me down." (See Chapter 13 - Ouija Board.) We all laughed at him and started back to our cars.

Leaving Jacksonville, we followed U.S. 17 and, driving along, we watched a Greyhound bus almost sideswipe the kids. They barely moved over to the shoulder of the road in time. I was panicky. I knew that was the second accident averted.

We continued on our journey, following the kids down the highway. Quite suddenly it occurred to me that I was seeing my vision. "Look, Pete," I said, "Look at their car; it's shimmering just like I told you that I saw last night. Toot the horn for them to pull over." Just as I made that statement, they almost ran off the road. As we pulled over too, they yelled that the hood of the car had flown up and blocked their view. Stew had to hold his head out of the window to see where they were going to guide Leon so they would not run off the road. Luckily, the pilot and co-pilot made a successful stop on the side of the road. The boys firmly tied the hood down with some rope so they would not have to worry about that anymore. Then, after Stew and Gary smoked about ten cigarettes to calm their nerves, we piled back into our cars and once again headed home. However, this time I relaxed, remembering only three black disks had flown from the car in my vision. I felt all the danger had passed since we had experienced three near-tragedies. The rest of the trip was happy and uneventful.

When we got home, tired and happy, and started getting ready for bed, we kept hearing a strange noise. Walking around looking for the cause, we discovered Pete's deceased grandmother's bedroom door was opening and closing by itself. We stood there, watched it and said out loud, "Granny, we love you but you are scaring us. Please leave your door open." She did, and that didn't happen anymore.

What a day!!

CHAPTER 9

OUT OF BODY EXPERIENCES AND KARMA

It is such an unusual occurrence to have an out-of-body experience. One afternoon, extremely exhausted, I plopped down on the sofa to relax. Closing my eyes for only a moment I could see myself lying on the sofa. It was as though I was near the ceiling looking down at myself. I could see my closed eyes and my lips so still. I looked so restful and peaceful. Then it frightened me into reality. I hopped up quickly and told my children, who were sitting in the living room reading, what had happened. I was afraid that I was going to die or something. Next morning I woke up with a rash. So the doctor called the drug store and ordered some antihistamine for me. After a few doses, I was so drowsy that I could not stay awake. I slept all day on that same sofa, just as I had seen myself the day before.

One of our young military friends, Greg, had a crush on Kathleen. He was on his way home to California on leave when he had an awesome encounter. He was driving down the road alone at night when he had a strange feeling that he should look in the rear-view mirror. As he did he clearly saw Kathleen sitting in the back seat. He slammed on the brakes, pulled off the road, turned around and looked in the back seat again. Of course, she was not there. She was in Savannah, 3,000 miles away. He was such a nervous wreck that at the very next phone booth he stopped to call our house to see if everything was okay.

When he called, the family was sitting quietly in the living room. We were listening to some soft, classical music. Kathleen was positioned on the couch resting her head against her arms. She had just made a comment, "I hope Greg is okay, I worry about him driving alone at night." I answered the phone and he told me of his unnerving ordeal. He then asked if she was wearing a black sweater and black slacks. Glancing at her, I acknowledged that she was, indeed, so dressed. He was so upset that he stopped driving for the night.

We had a precious little dog, Maggie, who had been our pet for many years. One afternoon she was hit by a car and killed. We cried and cried. The children picked flowers from the yard and put them all over her small little grave. We lived on an acre of land, so we buried her in our back yard near a wooded area. Later that evening at dusk, Kathleen and Madeline were sitting on the back-porch steps looking at Maggie's grave, and they witnessed an apparition in Maggie's form walk out of the grave. They ran into the house, trembling, stuttering and crying, trying to tell me what they had seen. I believed them but Pete was a little doubtful. So we went onto the back porch and sat on the steps a little while. As twilight passed into more darkness, we were looking at the stars and the big full moon that was lighting up our yard. Pete nudged my arm and whispered for me to look at the little grave. On this extra-clear night a small luminous cloud suddenly appeared, floating just over Maggie's grave. It was almost sitting on the grave. Being a scientific person, Pete got up to investigate the occurrence. The girls came out and started toward the grave too. When they were about fifteen feet from it, the cloud started moving toward them. Terrified, I ran out and grabbed them, screaming. "Don't let it touch you, run to the house," I shrieked uncontrollably as I pushed them into the back door. I was suddenly overcome with the feeling that if they had come in contact with the cloud, something bad would have happened to them. Spooky, isn't it?

A *karma* is an inevitable result in the future because of acts done in a past life. I recall a significant example.

When my sister, Ann, was sixteen years old she was constantly being annoyed by a neighbor boy. His name was Carl and he really was a nice guy. He was crazy about her, and every day he would come and sit on our front porch and talk to Mother until Ann came home. She finally went to the movies with him but declared that she didn't want to go out with him any more. She was more interested in a real handsome fellow, whose name was Leroy. After all, she was a teenager.

Poor Carl, he kept telling our mother how much he loved Ann and just wanted to be in her company, and he continued his daily vigil. Ann became disgusted because he wouldn't go away. So when she saw him coming she would go into her bedroom with a book, shut the door and read until he left.

Soon World War II broke out. Carl came over to our house to say goodbye. He had joined the army; he wanted to be a paratrooper. Mother begged Ann to come out and tell Carl goodbye but she wouldn't. He told us that he would never love anyone more than he loved Ann.

Well, on D-Day in France, as the American troops began the invasion, Carl was killed in his jump. The whole neighborhood was upset, especially Ann, embarrassed by guilt for not even saying, "Good luck," or, "Hurry back," and knowing he loved her. But that oversight is part of growing up.

About thirty-four years later, happily married and the mother of two teenaged sons, she and her husband went on a vacation to Europe. While they were there, she thought about Carl. So she and her husband Jack decided to try to locate Carl's grave. At the American Military Cemetery in Normandy, France, they followed the instructions they had been given and located the White Cross that identified Carl's grave site. They took pictures and sent them to his family in Savannah.

The karma had been fulfilled. Since he had been buried in France, no one had ever visited his grave except the one person he professed to love the most. So many times he had come to see her. At last, how very happy he must have been watching her from above walk up to him.

This is truly an inconceivable finale. A karma finished in this life.

CHAPTER 10

SPIRIT PEDIATRICIAN/GHOST SOLDIER

When our children were growing up they had a wonderful pediatrician. He always seemed to be available when we needed him, but we never knew how *great* he really was until after his death.

One afternoon after I had cleaned the house I was so tired that I decided to rest for a few minutes. While I was stretched out, relaxing, a vision came to me. Suddenly in a far-off distance I saw a tiny person. The person was quickly coming toward me. As it grew nearer and larger I realized it was Dr. Emerson Ham. Somewhat surprised, I could feel my face muscles forming a smile. But he kept coming closer and closer until his face was right in mine, so close that all I could see was an eye . . . one *huge eye* . . . and it was beautiful. As I lay there with my eyes closed, my mind's eye studied his enormous eye. I could not imagine why I was seeing this. As I watched, the eye started backing away and so did Dr. Ham, then they both vanished.

I sat up rather abruptly and sought the company of my husband. "Honey, I saw Dr. Ham and he was trying to tell me something about an eye. But I can't figure out what he was telling me."

"Well, go call him up and ask him," he answered.

"I can't, he is dead," I reminded him.

Since Mary Anne had been under his care when he passed away, it must be something wrong with her eyes, I imagined. I asked Mary Anne if her eyes bothered her. With her negative response I then looked closely to check for redness and irritation but found nothing. I even made an eye chart to check her eyes.

"Mother, this is stupid," she said.

I was so disturbed by my vision that I could not shake it. Finally I called my ophthalmologist and made an appointment for her. Dr. Schultz asked if she was having problems. "No, I just thought it might be a good idea to have her checked since she's never had an eye exam," I told him. After all, I could hardly say my deceased pediatrician sent me.

After the tests were completed Dr. Schultz announced that she had perfect vision. Thankfully I told him, "I knew this was a foolish trip but I am happy to know that she is okay."

"No, I am glad that you brought her in because she has a bad irritation behind her eyeballs. Does she swim in polluted water?"

"No, only in a neighbors pool," I answered.

"Well does a dog swim in the pool?"

"No they don't have a dog."

"Well no more swimming for a while," he commanded as he wrote her a prescription.

Stunned, we returned home. The family was in disbelief. How in the world could Dr. Ham know all that? But then he wasn't from this world any more. What a miracle! Who would believe it? Perhaps no one. I would love to share this with his family but am afraid they would think I was nuts. Maybe someday I will get the nerve to tell his son, who is also a doctor.

Several days later our neighbor came over to ask if we had seen his missing pet python snake. We didn't know he even had a snake. But believe me, I was careful around my shrubbery. I am terrified of snakes.

A little later when I saw the neighbors' children I inquired if they had found their snake. "Yes ma'am, he was in our swimming pool; he hides there sometime, he likes the water." My God, no wonder Mary Anne had an eye infection. She never was allowed to swim there again. I was relieved that this matter was finally resolved. Thank you, Dr. Ham! How proud your son would be to know you are still practicing medicine from the *Other Side*.

Bruce, a young neighborhood friend, had joined the Army during the Vietnam War. While he was home on leave, before going to the War Zone, he came by our house.

He was fascinated at a display of sea shells and shark's teeth we had collected. We explained the Corps of Engineers were dredging the Savannah River in order to deepen the channel. So they were pumping the silt out of the river bottom onto the shore to be used as landfill. The landfill site was on President Street Extension. We learned that lots of people had been out there searching for shark's teeth and fossils. So we had gone there and found lots of them too.

Bruce asked if we would take him next time, and we did. He was so thrilled with the shark's teeth he had found. He was going to have a hole drilled in one, he said, and wear it on his chain around his neck with his G.I. "dog tags" when he went to Vietnam. "It should bring me good luck," he laughed.

Six months went by. Bruce wrote that if he stayed another six months they would promote him to captain. After he got his new captain's bars, he had pictures taken in full-dress uniform and sent one to us. He was so proud of himself and so were we.

Several days after we received his picture we had a phone call. He had been killed when his helicopter exploded and there were no survivors. Two weeks later the whole neighborhood, it seemed, went to his funeral. The cemetery is located at Thunderbolt on the Wilmington River, high upon the bluff. After the service we stood next to his mother, waiting to speak to her. Most of the people had moved back a few feet when suddenly, from out of nowhere, a soldier in full-dress uniform appeared. He was standing right in front of us. He addressed his full attention to Bruce's mother and said, "I was with your son on his last mission and I just wanted you to know he was a fine and brave man." He saluted, turned and walked away.

I told Madeline to quickly get Bruce's two best friends that were standing near us because I know they would want to talk with this soldier. When we turned around he was gone. *He was not there at all*. The cemetery consists of about ten acres. It was impossible that anyone could have left without being seen: very few trees, very few bushes and only one road out. No people had even gotten into their cars yet. We asked everyone there, "Did you see where that soldier went?" Each and every one of them stated that they had not even seen a soldier. Only the six of us that had been standing together waiting to speak to Bruce's mother had seen him. No one believed us because the correspondence from the Army stated that there had been *no survivors*. Yet this person said he had been with Bruce on his last flight. He came, but disappeared. No sign of him. He had to have been a ghost. It is literally and physically impossible to leave that cemetery without being seen or heard. We were dumbfounded.

Mary Anne (age ten at that time) and I went home. As we closed the door Mary Anne turned toward me, threw her arms around me and broke down, sobbing her little heart out. Bruce had always paid a lot of attention to her, so she really was upset. As we stood there motionless, crying and hugging each other, something fell from the ceiling, and hit Mary Anne on the top of her head and then fell to the floor. We stooped down to pick it up and found one big shark's tooth. "Mother, Bruce is here!" She trembled as we both made a quick exit to the front porch. He loves us, I reassured her, but she was so afraid that she slept between Pete and I for a few nights.

CHAPTER 11

SMALL MIRACLES

Our three daughters are very close to each other. None of them had ever been away from home, so when Kathleen married and left, it was traumatic for her sisters. She had moved 9,000 miles away to Anchorage, Alaska, where her husband was stationed in the Army.

One morning I sat up in bed, crying my eyeballs out.

"What in the world is the matter with you?" Pete asked.

"Kathleen is crying, something is wrong with her," I said.

"Now, what makes you think that?"

"I saw her and could hear her crying."

Jumping out of bed, I hurried to the telephone. "Who are you calling at this hour, its only 6 o'clock?" Pete inquired.

"I've got to call Kathleen,"

"They are still asleep, remember there's a five-hour time difference" he reminded me. Anxiously I waited and watched the clock. When I figured they were up, I quickly made the 9,000-mile phone call.

When she answered, she was crying. "Mama, Mama, I broke my jaw tooth, it split right down the middle, and I'm in such pain. I've been up all night crying; what can I do?" she sobbed.

I cried too. "Now, honey take your pain medicine the dentist gave you and keep hot compresses on your face, and maybe let you husband make you some warm tea, and be sure you don't go out in the cold or snow," I suggested. Reminding each other of our devoted love and Kathleen's reassuring me she felt better since we had both talked, we finally hung up.

Several months later Madeline had a high temperature and a bad throat infection, so I took her to Dr. Robert. He gave her some penicillin which she took for several days. Feeling a little better, she went back to school. The next day her 104° fever returned. Panicked, I phoned the doctor, and he instructed us to take her to the Emergency Room and let the resident physician look at her. I wasn't too happy with his instructions, letting another doctor attend to her, but we went. All they did at the hospital was to give her a walloping shot of penicillin again, and then we took her home.

That night I had a vision. I was standing in a hospital corridor with my doctor, Dr. Straight, outside a room where Madeline was supposedly in a bed. The doctor said to me, "If you don't watch her carefully she will have brain damage or she might not make it at all." This was very upsetting, and for a while I put it out of my mind because in the vision it was the wrong doctor. Dr. Robert was her physician, not Dr. Straight.

Around noon the next day Madeline broke out in a horrible rash. She was covered from head to toe, and her temperature again had climbed to 104° We called her own doctor, but he was "out for the day." So Pete and I bundled her up and took her to my doctor (the one in my vision). I was so upset I didn't even think about that, at the time. He immediately sent her to the hospital. He said she had strep throat; evidently penicillin had not touched the infection. He then changed her medication to Erythromycin. Her fever was then 106° and her condition was very critical. Then she developed a terrible reaction to that drug also. She looked like someone who had been baked in the sun for hours and had purple dots on top of that. I believe every nurse and doctor in the hospital, whether out of care or curiosity, came to see her.

On the seventh day, I was still sitting by her bed. I had not left her room since she was admitted. The nurse came in and started a new IV. I sat there for a while watching the drip-drip-drip when suddenly I noticed way up in the tube an air pocket about four inches long.

As I watched this air pocket get closer to Madeline's arm, my thoughts drifted back to a conversation I had with my father years ago. He told us about a friend who had very minor surgery but who went into a coma after she had an air embolism enter her blood stream from a simple intravenous infusion. I jumped to my feet and rang for the nurse. "Please come bleed the air pocket from my daughter's IV," I requested.

"Okay," she answered. I waited and watched the air pocket moving. The nurse never came back, so I called again. "Please come here, the air is almost to her arm," I said nervously. The door opened and the nurse came in. She looked at the tube. "It's okay . . . it won't hurt anything," she said.

"I do not want that air to go into her bloodstream," I demanded as she walked out of the room. I was very upset. I knew if I allowed the air to go into her vein, she would die. What could I do? Well, as it approached her wrist I pinched the tube off with my fingers and allowed no more fluid to come through. For twenty minutes or so I clamped it, then the door opened and in came our doctor. He was so-o-o mad when he heard the story. He very quickly scolded the nurse, and told her she should have known better. She *did* bleed it then.

Dr. Straight told me I had better call Kathleen and tell her to come home from Alaska because he did not know if Madeline would survive. Her temperature still remained 106° and she was almost comatose. Pete and I called. "If she is no better in the morning, you had better come," I said tearfully. Needless to say, Kathleen was overcome with emotion. I cried all night. Deborah, Madeline's friend, came up to the hospital to spend the night with us.

Madeline lay very still. When Dr. Straight came in the room the next morning, he walked over to her, put his hand on her forehead and smiled a huge smile. "She has passed the crisis, her fever is gone, she will be all right." We all hugged, kissed and cried. Leaving Deborah with Madeline, Pete and I ran to the phone to call Kathleen. When her husband answered the phone he expressed delight at the news. Then he told us that after we had phoned the night before, Kathleen was so upset she ran to her bedroom crying and knelt down beside her bed and talked with God and begged him to give Madeline's illness to her because she felt she was stronger and could handle it better than Madeline. He told us Kathleen had gotten very weak and she suddenly had a temperature of 105° all night, but she was now normal, but exhausted.

Crisis!

Miracle?

Did God really answer the prayers of a young girl begging for the life of her sister? Begging so hard, offering to take on the burden of the illness, or even share it with her sister? Strangely, the crisis was passed at the same time Kathleen's fever soared and apparently for no physical reason.

Yes, I will always *know* God does work small miracles when there is such devotion and unselfish love.

CHAPTER 12

PALMISTY

In 1968 Kathleen was a senior in high school. As part of an English assignment she had to write a term paper. The students could select any subject from the list the teacher had prepared and put on the board, things such as E.S.P, palmistry, witchcraft and clairvoyance.

The reason the teacher gave for compiling such a strange variety of subjects was to force the young people to do research. However, the teacher did not know about the strange happenings at our house. Kathleen decided to do her paper on clairvoyance. She wanted to include an interview with me in her report, but she also needed book references. So off to the library we went.

While waiting for her to make her selections, I came across some books on palmistry. I laughed and thought to myself, *this is ridiculous!* I always associated palm reading with gypsies. And, of course, I could not make myself believe people can look at a palm and tell you what has transpired in your past and what will take place in the future. But out of mere curiosity I checked out several of these books.

Although I do not enjoy cuddling up at night with a book, I found myself totally captivated. I read not only in the evening but also while I was cooking, washing clothes, taking a bath . . . just all the time. These books were fascinating. They showed a multitude of handprints, and with each set of prints, they explained all the special lines and marks, and went into depth as to the variety of meanings.

For fun I would choose a particular line in the book that

intrigued me. Then I would look on anyone's hand that the particular line would have meaning, and it always seemed to fit. So I matched most lines to real-life persons, and they applied properly. We were having a ball with this new venture, and were starting to believe that it really had some truth to it, when I found a very upsetting mark on the hand of someone I love very much. It was a sign that upset me tremendously. (I prefer at this time not to disclose what this secret is, because the person concerned in the matter does not know about it. There are only three people who know my secret.)

Because of this discovery I have studied palmistry in an effort to prove it was a bunch of *phooey* . . . to prove that there is absolutely nothing to it at all. So I have pursued this study with a negative attitude, trying desperately to disprove any truth associated with palmistry.

In my desire to fully understand this "science," I have read every book I could find concerning this subject. Every time I've gone near a bookstore I have sought out new books and purchased them. For the past twenty-five years I have studied this art and applied it to my family and friends and have even read palms for some strangers. In no instance have I been able to prove one mark or line to be incorrect.

Look at your hands. No two hands are the same. No two sets of fingerprints are the same. Have you ever heard the Biblical term *It Is Written*? Well, I believe this applies to each individual life. I firmly believe that God has written his plans for my life in my hands and yours in your hands. Certainly God does not have all this down on paper, that would be an absurd thought. He gave it to us in our hands. These lines and marks can change sometimes . . . or even disappear. The studies all tell us that the left hand is what God intended our life to be and the right hand is the changes we are allowed to make. Note that I said "allowed to make." Let me explain. If there is a special mark on both hands, for example such as an accident, and it shows in both hands at the same age, then it is inevitable. However, if one are aware of the warning, he could be extra careful during this period of life and possibly avert a tragedy by turning the situation into a more minor accident. If the mark is only on one hand, then by being cautious at that age, one can completely avoid the whole problem.

At this point I would like to mention a few incidents that helped me to become a believer. In May of 1975, I had been studying the major lines for several weeks when I saw a mark on my "life line" that meant surgery. Going over to the kitchen sink where the light was better, I yelled for Pete.

"Come here, Honey!"

"What's up?" he asked.

"I have surgery marks on both hands." I held my palms so he could see them.

"Don't worry, you feel fine, don't you?" he laughed.

"Yes."

"Well, then, what's the big deal?"

"But you don't understand, honey; if I had the surgery mark (which is, incidentally, an "X" on the "life line") on one hand it would mean an operation with complete recovery. But, since it is on both hands in the exact place, it means 'surgery' with possibility of death."

Pete hugged and kissed me. "Don't worry about all that stuff; you know its just a bunch of malarkey." I worried about this for a few days and then put it out of my head.

A few weeks later I was hot and tired. I had been raking in the yard. When I went into the house, I flopped down across my bed and closed my eyes. I was home alone. All the children had gone to school. As I was lying there letting my mind wonder over the past events of the morning, I very clearly heard a man's voice say to me, "Your life is in danger." That's all! The statement was very smooth but also very positive. The voice appeared to be that of a thirty-five-year-old man. I really do not know why that particular age stays in my mind, but it does. I was terrified. I jumped from my bed and ran to check the doors, for I was sure a man had gotten in the house. All the doors were secure, but I was in a cold sweat. Had I heard a spirit speak to me? I decided to go back outside and continue my work. I mentioned this to the family, but , as per usual, in a day or so we dismissed it from our minds.

On June 22 about 8:30 a.m., I was hurrying around the house trying to go to help Mary, my good sister-like friend. We were taking care of the nursery in the church's Vacation Bible School. Suddenly out of the clear blue sky, I had a terrible pain in my tummy. I could hardly move. I went to the phone, "Hello, Mary, I sure hate to let you down but I feel terrible; I don't know why but my stomach is killing me." (I didn't know it then, but that was exactly what was happening; it was literally killing me).

"Don't worry about Bible School; you just get to feeling better. You probably have the virus that is going around," Mary replied.

In less than an hour my two oldest daughters had put me in the car and headed to the Emergency Room of the Candler Hospital. I was in screaming pain and kept passing out. After I was admitted I lay in a semi-conscious state for eight days hooked up to IVs, catheters and tubes running down my throat to keep me from vomiting. The doctors ran all kinds of tests but could not find the problem. Pete was nearly crazy at this point because I had never been sick in my life, and here I was dying before his very eyes. That morning he insisted that our doctor call in a consultant.

Now, while all this was taking place, I wasn't aware of anything around me. However, at my lowest point in this crisis, I had a vision. I remember that I thought I was standing under a huge, very ornate golden arch. It was the beginning of a very, very long corridor, with a multitude of identical golden vaulted arches. At the very end of this corridor was the most beautiful brilliant light I've ever seen. It seemed to be beckoning to me to come toward it. I could faintly hear beautiful music that appeared to be coming from the same direction as the luminous point.

I felt compelled to step through the archway and start

toward the light, for I knew I would no longer be in pain but at peace, and I would be embraced by the loving arms of my Savior, Jesus Christ, if only I could be engulfed by the light's brilliance. As I started in my mind to take the first step, my subconscious self must have taken over, for I remember shaking my head violently and yelling out loud, "No! No! No! I have too much to do, I don't want to go now." Then I opened my eyes to see my family gathered around me asking what was wrong. I told them I had had a vision. Then I lapsed back into semi-consciousness.

In my heart I knew if I had taken that one step through the archway, there would have been no return to this world, for I knew it was an invitation from the Lord to come to him if I was ready. My only regret is that I could never share with anyone the astronomical beauty of such an experience and what I had the privilege to see. There is no way to recapture the moment and no way to explain it. But when I relive it from time to time, I become filled with emotion and wonderment.

My physician, Dr. George Straight, called in a well-known surgeon, Dr. Tom Freeman. After their consultation they decided to operate the next day. I can hardly remember anything about those eight days. I do recall my mother saying to me, "Look who is here." When I opened my eyes, I saw my sister Ann standing by my side. I could suddenly feel a sense of courage sweep over me. Then I noticed my nephews, William and Randy, standing by the door with very serious looks on their faces. They even looked somewhat scared.

The doctors aroused me to explain about the surgery. I was very upset and started to cry. My very sweet mother was sitting with me at the time. "Mama, I'm scared. If only Leon could be with me now I know I'd be all right." Leon was my brother. We were always each other's strengths when we were children, and I really needed him now. But he was in New Jersey getting ready to do another tour of duty in Vietnam. As soon as someone came to relieve Mama, unbeknown to me, she beat it down to the Red Cross Chapter House to get an emergency leave for him. The Army let him fly home to be with the family. I only remember seeing him for a brief second before the nurses took me to the operating room. Then after my surgery, when I came to, Leon was telling me he had to leave, and I remember I started to cry, and he leaned over and kissed me and he started crying too as he took his wings off his uniform and pinned them on my gown. In a few minutes he was gone, on his way to Vietnam, but his presence had helped me pull through the surgery.

I almost didn't make it. They found an intestine had kinked. Gangrene set in, then the intestine had ruptured. So I also had peritonitis. It was "touch and go" for awhile, but I had a multitude of friends and family praying for me. The surgeon said, "It was now up to the Lord."

A soaring temperature came over my body, and once again I lay flat on my back, slipping away, greatly tired, all my defenses exhausted. Then another little miracle happened. Through the door walked my tiny adorable little girl, who was only seven years old. We had not seen each other for two weeks. She could not understand what was happening. My precious Mary Anne climbed upon a stool the nurse had placed by my bed. "Oh, God, my baby needs me." She was hugging and kissing me and crying her little heart out. While I felt her tiny hands patting my face and her warm tears falling on my cheeks, it was as if an angel had touched me, and I felt a new inner peace engulf me. I felt bathed in new found energy. From that moment on I improved by leaps and bounds.

My condition improved. I was napping. Kathleen and Madeline were on the right side of my bed holding my hand, and my daddy was on my left, holding my other hand. All of a sudden I felt a very cool female hand gently pat my shoulder on bare skin as though to say, "You're going to be all right."

I quickly opened my eyes and inquired, "Did anybody touch me on my shoulder?"

"No," they all three replied simultaneously. I will always

believe that it was Ruth's spirit reassuring me.

Several weeks after I was home I remembered about the palmistry. I could hardly believe the accuracy which my hand had predicted all my health problems. I decided to take another look at my palms.

About a ¼ of an inch from the first "x" was another pair of "x's" on both hands, indicating more serious surgery with the possibility of death. Frantically, I showed them to Pete and I said, "Promise me if I have to go back to the hospital, you won't allow the doctors to give me anything to make me sleepy or dopey. Because I have to be awake so I can help save myself."

"Okay," he promised.

Exactly six months later, on the morning of December 15, I woke up to find a big lump protruding from my abdomen about where an appendix would be, and it was extremely tender. We called my doctor and he ordered me straight to the hospital. All the way there I cried, "Please promise me you won't let the doctor dope me up, if they do I might die, promise me, promise me." So the first thing Pete did when he saw my *great* surgeon was to demand on my behalf that I not, at any time, be sedated. (He didn't tell him why because he might have thought that I needed to be in the psychiatric ward if I had said, "My palm tells me my life is in danger.") The doctor was determined that I had a large abscess and decided to treat me with high-powered antibiotics to see if they could clear up the infection without surgery.

The next morning I got up and walked to the bathroom, and as I came out, the doctor was standing in my room. I told him I could hardly urinate. Surprised at this, he examined me once again, and, much to his disbelief, he discovered that the abscess had grown from the size of an egg to the size of a grapefruit. He scheduled surgery for that same afternoon to remove the abscess. The next day I was told that if I had been groggy and unable to tell them about the urinary problem, the abscess would have burst, and I would have probably died.

Seven days later I went home. So by using the knowledge I had gained about palmistry, I am certain I saved my own life. I was told that in six months I would have to go back to the hospital for repair surgery. So searching my palm closely one more time, I could see one last X, but it was only on one hand. So, when the time came for the repair job, I went in happily and in good spirits because I knew this time I would be just fine.

Now, I would not suggest running out and finding a palmistry book, because it can be dangerous to an amateur. For example, seeing a mark that indicates illness on someone's hand without knowing that the divine protection mark was on the other hand to contradict the seriousness of the situation might create, by the power of suggestion, a tragic happening. I feel one must have some form of a psychic gift to define it all and apply it accurately.

I also feel that to study this scientific art is not un-Christian, for it is God himself that made every part of each of us, including our hands and their lines. If one attains this knowledge and uses his ability to help people, then I feel in my heart God would not frown. However, to use this gift for profit would be wrong. Maybe I am wrong but, that is what my conscience dictates.

I have always found it difficult to be objective about my own hand. So I wanted to find someone who could read it for me. Several licensed palmists, or so they claimed, came to town. The first one I visited told me to think of two things I wanted to know, and she'd advise me. Then she had me touch the center of my left palm with the index finger of my right hand. I did this. She then asked me what I wanted to know. When I told her I was concerned for a relative's health, she said she could cure my relative, provided I give her $90.00. There was no charge for the cure, she said, the money was for special candles that had to be ordered from another country that she used for offering special prayers. I told her I didn't have that kind of money so I would have to talk to her later. Of course, I never went back!

Two months later I went to another palmist. She was a very young and attractive woman. She had me do the same thing as the first palmist. She gave me the "pitch" about the $90.00 worth of candles so she could pray over them. I could hardly believe this. So I told her I did not come there for counseling; I wanted her to read the lines on my hand. She was floored by my request and admitted that she couldn't read lines. She only saw pictures in the middle of a person's hand. I told her that I dabbled in palmistry and had read for several people, but that I was unable to read my own hands.

Outstretching her own hand to reveal her palm, she asked me about her lines (of course, I knew she was testing me.) I asked her, "Do you really want to know what I see?" She nodded affirmatively. So here I am sitting in a palmist's office reading her palm. "How dumb," I thought. I showed her three islands on her life line that meant periods of ill health. But I assured her she would recover fully each time. Then, glancing at her other hand for a moment, I told her about her two marriages and unhappy sex life, which she openly admitted was true. Once again I assured her betterment was ahead in the near future. I then paid her $5.00 and left. I laughed all the way home. My family thought this was hysterical.

After I had been home for a while I was thinking over the events of the afternoon when I realized something important. I dashed to the phone, and on the other end this deep mysterious voice said, "Madam Bella speaking."

"Hi, I'm the lady that was there a little while ago and read your palm."

"Oh, yes, I remember," she replied.

"Well I was just thinking about you and a thought came to me. I wanted to mention that each of your illnesses will be corrected through surgery, but don't worry, you'll get along fine."

"Thank you for calling, and come see me again soon," she said.

I won't, I thought as I hung up.

The reason I am relating this is so that you will not be taken in by false prophets. Most of these people are not really reaching out to help people, but to take you for an expensive ride. I do have to mention something that often makes me laugh. When I first started reading palms, I mentioned it to my sister Ann. We went to Florida to see her and her family. When we arrived, her two little boys, William and Randy, had been eating lunch and had peanut butter and jelly on their faces. They ran out to the car, thrust both their hands at me and said excitedly, "Aunt Mil, read our hands!"

Smilingly I took one of both of their hands and said, "Hum-m-m, I see by your hands you have been eating peanut butter and jelly."

They were amazed, and as they walked away wiping their mouths on their shirt sleeves, I could hear them say, "Wow, wonder how she knew that?"

A young friend of ours came over and said, "It is so stupid to think you can tell the future by looking at your hand," he declared. "Read mine," he added jokingly.

I looked quickly, and not trying to be serious, I told him, "Be careful, I see a head injury. I don't know how you will get it but be careful."

He laughed all the way out the door, almost in hysterics. "Dumb, dumb, dumb," he was saying.

Two weeks later I got a phone call from his mother, "I'm at work and I don't have a car. Is there anyway you could please go to Savannah High School and pick up Alvin and take him to the doctor for me? The school called and said he was hurt."

"Sure will, no problem," I answered.

While sitting in the doctor's office, it suddenly occurred to Alvin about the palm reading. "I can't believe this," he muttered as he held a wad of gauze to his bleeding head that required several stitches.

He said he was in shop at school making a surf board. Another boy came up and said, "I think you have my surf board," and when Alvin told him it was his own, the boy picked up a board and beat him in the head.

CHAPTER 13

OUIJA BOARD

In June of 1985 my mother called to my attention an article in the newspaper about a Ouija Board accurately predicting the outcome of a famous horse race. Also, it had correctly named the man who would win the election for mayor of New York City. This was hard to believe because a Ouija Board is just a simple piece of board bearing the alphabet, numbers zero through nine and the word "yes" in one corner and "no" in the opposite corner. Also it comes with a planchet, a plastic heart-shaped object with a circle of clear plastic in the middle to allow one to see the letters or numbers on which it stops.

We have had a Ouija Board around the house for years collecting dust. One of the children had received it for Christmas a while back. We never played with it because I thought the children had to push it to get the answers they wanted and that wasn't any fun. How could some $3.98 game make real predictions?

"Get out the Ouija Board, kids," I laughed. The directions said for two people to face each other, knees together and touching, place the Board on both of their laps, then place the planchet in the middle of the board. Each player should put his or her fingers very lightly on the planchet. Then, according to superstition, ask a question and a spirit moves the disk from letter to letter to give a message.

Kathleen, seventeen by then, gave her word that she would not push. We asked all kinds of stupid questions and got equally silly answers. Hey, this was interesting! The only thing, though, was that it would not work for anyone except Kathleen and me. We had lots of friends and neighbors come over to observe, or to participate and have fun. We would laugh for hours.

We would ask, "What spirit pushes this board?"

"Ruth," it spelled. *Lordy me, we're talking to Aunt Ruth.*

"Why did you come to live with us, Ruth?" we asked.

"Because you have fun."

"Is it you who opens the utility room door?" we asked.

"Who else?" it replied.

Danny, a young Italian neighbor boy came by one evening while a bunch of us were engrossed in our Ouija Board. He brought a really cute girlfriend with him. Suddenly the Ouija Board said, "Show that girl what a Latin lover you are." We were all embarrassed, but we never knew what the Board was going to say.

Dickie, my nephew, also came over that same evening and while the Ouija Board was in the middle of a sentence, Dickie said, "Why are you playing with that stupid thing?"

Abruptly the disk stopped dead still and then suddenly jerked to the letters, "Shut up Jackass." Amid the hysterical laughter, a shocked and red-faced Dickie went to sit quietly in a corner of the room.

Norman, our good friend but more like a brother, declared, "I don't believe all this. You are pushing the disk." We reassured him that we didn't, but to prove our point Kathleen and I closed our eyes and allowed Norman to put cotton balls on our eyelids. Then he took a large cloth and blindfolded us. As if that weren't enough, he turned the board around so we wouldn't have any idea what the letters and numbers were. Then he asked out loud, "Okay, do you have anything you would like to tell us, Aunt Ruth?"

Quickly, it rushed to the word "yes." Then the planchet moved smoothly to different letters. We always had someone write down the letters so we could read the message. This message read, "Kathleen, look behind the head of your bed for a red box, you will find something you have been looking for."

As Norman read this out loud, we jerked off our blindfolds and practically flew to the bedroom. Kathleen and nine other people were on hands and knees looking under the bed. There it was: a very small red box. Opening it very carefully, she peeked inside and shrieked with pleasure. Sure enough there were the two pictures of her and Madeline sitting on Santa Claus's lap. They'd had them made for Christmas for their father and me but could not remember where they had hid them. Everyone was in disbelief because these pictures had been missing for two months!

Back to the Ouija Board, hands in place, Kathleen said, "Thanks, Aunt Ruth."

Norman was giggling nervously about all of this, so he announced, "Well, I'd better be going as I have a long road ahead of me." He lived across the Savannah River in Hardeville, South Carolina. Then, being a smart-aleck, he laughed, "Bye-bye, Aunt Ruth."

The planchet started moving and spelled out, "Meet you at the bridge."

Norman was truly shaken and turned white as a visible ghost. As we all laughed uncontrollably at him, he said, stuttering slightly, "Uh-h-h, I think I'll just spend the night here." Now, who in his right mind would like to drive thirty miles on a dark, moonless night alone at midnight, knowing a spirit was going to meet him at a bridge that crosses over a river and then a swamp? Not Norman! How about you?

We had two parakeets. Their names were Goldie and Barnabus. We had their cage hanging by the back door where the birds could get lots of sunlight. They sang and chirped all day. Goldie was a beautiful yellow bird; Barnabus was blue. We named him after a vampire named Barnabus Collins from the television program *Dark Shadows*.

One afternoon the birds were chirping contentedly when suddenly Goldie shrieked and fluttered violently around the cage and dropped dead while Barnabus, seemingly terrified, stood on his perch and never moved. Maybe a big roach got into the cage and frightened her to death, but why not Barnabus? We were all sad and concerned.

That evening when all of our young neighborhood friends came over, it was suggested that we ask Aunt Ruth about Goldie on the Ouija Board. As Kathleen and I began, we asked, "Do you know why Goldie died?"

"Yes, she was scared to death," it replied.

"Well, what scared her?" Kathleen asked.

"Me," said Ruth (supposedly).

"Well why didn't you scare Barnabus?" I questioned.

Believe it or not, the reply was, "I don't mess around with vampires!"

My nephews, William and Randy, were visiting us from Orange City, Florida. "Let's play Ouija Board, Aunt Mil," they pleaded.

They were overly anxious as we got started, but the only message we got was "Tell Mama, tell Mama, tell Mama." This did not sound like it was Ruth. Maybe it was a child spirit. It would not talk to us. It only kept pointing out "OP 6 RT 10" then a series of numbers came up.

We thought we were just getting some silly mumbo jumbo when the telephone rang. "Mrs. Martin, please," the lady on the other end said.

"She is not here, but she will be back in a few minutes," we told her.

"Have her call Operator 6 in California," she requested.

When Mother got home she read the note we had jotted down for her: "Call Operator 6." Wow, we thought! Quickly returning the call, she found it was my brother, Leon, in California. He phoned to tell us he was leaving California for home and wanted us to know that he was taking Route 10 and gave us his license tag number so that in case of an emergency we could find him. His license tag numbers were the same numbers that had been coming across the Ouija Board. He said he was in a hurry, and his friends were waiting on him, but he said, "I told them I had to tell Mama." This made staunch believers of William and Randy. Was that mental telepathy or was the spirit in California traveling more than 3,000 miles in a matter of minutes to deliver his message? Even the most modern jets do not fly that fast.

One rainy afternoon Stew came over with a couple of friends. He dragged out the Ouija Board to show them, and we started playing. Before we could ask it any questions it pointed out, "I'm a better sword fighter than you, Stew!"

"Oh, my God, that was Aunt Ruth who knocked me off the bench at the Jacksonville Zoo!" exclaimed a petrified Stew.

Then the planchet wrote, "Ha, Ha, Ha." (Remember Chapter 8, the trip to Florida? Stew was clowning around, pretending to sword fight with an invisible person when he fell off the bench and said it felt like somebody pushed him down? Well, that day we learned that Ruth had gone with us.)

Betty, a friend of mine, went to a Tupperware party. Somehow the conversation got around to discussing Ouija Boards and whether people or spirits moved the disk. Betty guaranteed everybody she had seen an invisible source move it, and that we call our invisible source Aunt Ruth.

She excused herself from the company and went to the phone. "Hello, Mildred, are you busy?" she asked.

"Just watching a little television," I said.

"Is there anyway you and Kathleen could bring your Ouija Board over here so I can prove to all these women that it's for real?"

"Okay, we'll be there in a few minutes," I answered.

Arriving, Ouija Board in hand, we entertained the group for half an hour. The board was very active, and everybody asked questions, all receiving reasonable replies. Then one of the women's husbands arrived, and he was making fun of us in a very humiliating tone. His wife told him to say something to the Board. He belly laughed, "Hello, Ruth."

Immediately with very strong jerking strokes, Ruth replied,

"Hey, Stupid."

He left in a huff, thinking we had done it! But we hadn't, and as we left to go home, everyone was still roaring with laughter.

A week after Christmas, but still during the holidays, our teenaged girls and their friends wanted to have a party. They wanted to invite about twenty-five young people, but our house was a little small for such a crowd, especially for dancing. However, Pete's father was living with his sister since his wife had died. We made a quick call and got permission to have our party at his house. They had no Christmas decorations, but it was only four blocks from our house so three of the boys, Ken, Dickie and Gary, carried our tree there to Papa's house. It was so funny watching two of them walking down the street carrying our seven-foot tree, all decorated with lights, tinsel, colored balls and a star on top! The third guy was walking alongside of them carrying the electric cord. We hurried there in the cars, turned on the furnace, lit the fireplace, turned on the music, and the fun began!

Pete and I had made one stipulation: no alcohol. There were several boys who were old enough to have a beer on occasion, but since the crowd consisted of younger teenagers also, we wanted to make sure their parents knew no alcohol would be served . . . only Cokes, popcorn, chips and dips. The dancing lasted for hours. Then, in front of the fireplace, the group was singing when the inevitable happened. "Look at what I brought," someone yelled. Oh, no! The Ouija Board had arrived.

The group went silent as we asked, "Aunt Ruth, are you here? Did you come to our party?"

The Ouija Board was still, no movement.

"Will you talk to us?" one of the youngsters begged.

Very slowly the planchet began moving. It spelled out, "Jack Daniels is here."

There is no one here with that name, we answered out loud.

"In the kitchen, Greg brought it," it wrote. I jumped up and ran into the kitchen, only to see Pete and Greg mixing a drink. On the counter was a bottle of Jack Daniels whiskey. Greg was twenty-four years old, and he had brought the bottle for Pete and him to have a quiet drink together, but he was respectful enough not to let the teenagers see it. So he had come in the back door, and nobody would have ever known it except for (excuse the expression) Ruth's big mouth. I say that jokingly, of course!

Next, we all settled back down and started again. However, we discovered that the clear plastic circle in the middle of the disk had fallen out. As we placed our hands on the planchet Pete walked over to us and slid a piece of paper on the Board. Then he placed a magic marker in the hole where the plastic had been. Then he announced, "Okay, Ruth, if you are so smart write somethin'" . . . he pronounced it without the "g."

Sure enough, the disk started dragging the marker very quickly, and it wrote the word *somethin* just as Pete had told her to do, eliciting laughter from everyone.

Then he turned the paper over and said, "Whoever you are, write your name."

Instantly it wrote in cursive: *Ruth.* We were so excited!

We got another paper which was as big as the entire Ouija Board. Once again Pete held the tip end of the marker in the hole. We waited a few minutes then, at rapid speed, it drew lines all over the paper from one side to the other.

"It's not writing anything, its just scribbling," someone said. Then it abruptly came to a stop. When we removed the planchet we realized that it had drawn a picture of a house but we could not identify it.

Turning the paper over again, we asked "Whose house is this?"

It then wrote in a box letter style, "new addition."

Astonished, we realized this was for the back of our home. We had recently added on a huge bedroom for our daughters along with a big den. We were having the renovations made so we could move in as soon as we sold our existing house. The picture showed the sliding glass doors, the back door . . . even the chimney with smoke coming out. Also the tree near the breakfast room!

Bewildered, we decided we had better not play this *game* any more. It had started scaring all of us.

As time marched on I was cleaning around the house, and I unearthed the Ouija Board. "Come on, Kathleen, lets play one last time," I requested. Reluctantly, she agreed.

This time no claim was made as to who was moving the disk. "Is there a spirit here that wants to tell us something?"

Nothing appeared for a minute or two, then these words came out of my mouth, "Have I ever lived before?"

Immediately the disk raced to the word "yes."

Being very surprised, I asked, "what was my name?"

It very slowly spelled out the name *Gereber.*

Then we asked, "What year did this person live?"

It wrote back: *467.*

"What did this person do," we asked.

"Priest and Teacher."

"What did he teach?" I inquired.

"Taught people to love one another," it wrote.

We put the Ouija Board away, somewhat bewildered. Could this be true? I wonder! Jokingly everyone started calling me, "Gereber."

I have read from several different church-related articles that it is not safe to use a Ouija Board. There is a chance of picking up a bad spirit. So I no longer recommend it as a parlor game, even though it was fun. We were lucky we did not pick up a bad spirit, and we will always hope that Aunt Ruth was having fun with us. But we have retired the Ouija Board for good, especially since we discovered the church discourages its use.

Incidentally, when we got home from the Christmas Party, we looked in my mother's Bible where she kept the last Christmas card Ruth had sent her before she died. The signature on the card matched the name that the spirit had written through the Ouija Board.

WEIRD!

CHAPTER 14

GEREBERNUS

Shortly after Christmas we moved from Wilmere to Skidaway Road, the old family home. Before we moved in, we had cleaned out the closets and wiped the shelves with a damp rag. About a year later, I went into my bedroom closet to get a purse off the shelf overhead, and as I dragged down the purse, something fell on my head and then onto the floor. When I picked it up, much to my complete astonishment, it was a medal like the ones the Catholics wear. The medal was made of an aluminum-type material. It had an engraved picture on it. When I examined it with my magnifying glass I almost fainted. The picture was of a man and it was inscribed *Saint Gerebernue*. In Latin it also said, "Pray for Us." On the other side was the image of a woman, inscribed *Saint Dymphna*. She was dressed like a queen and wore a crown on her head.

No one knew its origin; the family was mystified. How did it get there? Thinking it had to be a Catholic medal, we asked six different priests if they had ever heard of Gerebernus or Saint Dymphna. Not even the bishop had heard of either.

Finally one evening we were visiting Aunt Helen and telling her this story. She suggested that we look them up in her family Catholic encyclopedias, which were written in 1907. When I located Gerebernus' name it referred me to the book of Dymphna. As I turned to that particular page, a four-leaf clover dropped to my feet from out of the book. Aunt Helen said she didn't know it was in there. It was as if someone was saying "good luck." A chilling feeling filled the room. Helen said it had been at least twenty years since anyone had looked up anything in these books.

Gerebernus and Dymphana were working with simple-minded people. Dymphana, "who was the daughter of a pagan king of Ireland, became a Christian and was secretly baptized. After the death of her mother, her father desired to marry his own daughter, so she ran away with the priest, Gerebernus, and landed at Antwerp, Belgium. They went on to the village of Gheel, where there was a Chapel of St. Martin, beside which they took up their abode. There they started a school for the simple-minded, continuing their life's dedication to teach those handicapped persons to help themselves." ("Dympna," *The Catholic Encyclopedia*, Vol. 5, The Encyclopedia Press, Inc., New York, Year 1909/1913)

A strange coincidence? These two people were working with the simple-minded (mentally handicapped). And at the time of this awakening, I was helping to teach a special-education class to the mentally retarded at my mother's church. I had been helping for a year and a half. Does all this seem strange? Some people believe you live more than one time and others don't. I *do*!

Perhaps if I lived other lives, I might have been Gerebernus. Who knows? Someday I hope to pursue my search for facts. I would like to make a trip to Gheel, Belgium, to see if there are any relics that might offer a clue.

As I was looking in the old encyclopedia today trying to be sure my information was accurate, I was once again astonished when I realized that the chapel in which they lived at Gheel was named St. Martin. Martin, being my maiden name, only emphasized my fascination all the more.

Analyzing all this and comparing it to my life today (in 1995), I am a caretaker. I have been at the Chatham Nursing Home almost everyday for the past fourteen years. I have become friends with hundreds of the residents and all of the staff. My very dear mother, who had Alzheimer's disease, lives there. I go every day to visit, to feed her, to roll her around and tuck her into bed. But most of all, each night I tell her what a good mother she has always been and how much I love her. Then I kiss her goodnight. Mother is ninety-four years old.

My brother was a patient there seven years before mother. Every day I was there to see about him. During this time, the special friends I have acquired are wonderful! Pam and Sandy are mentally great, but they have physical problems. We have become very close. One patient, who is retarded, has attached herself to me. She is about sixty-three. Every night she watches for me, and if I am a few minutes late, she worries. She goes with me to feed Mother, then we go for a walk. She calls mother "my baby." She has two dolls, and she pushes them around in a stroller each night with us. I just love her!

About two-thirds of the patients are confused. But when I am there just saying hello or chatting a few minutes, it makes each of them feel important and they smile. I try to tell them something funny to make them laugh. When I leave at night to come home, even if I am exhausted, I feel good inside and happy.

When I was a young girl about twelve years old, Mother would let me walk over to my grandmother's house. On the way I would pass by a nursing home called "Little Sisters of the Poor." Some of the elderly men and women were sitting on a porch in big rocking chairs. The home was huge, and it was enclosed by a giant red brick fence. I always felt sorry for the old folks. They looked so lonely.

I remember one afternoon I paused at their entrance, and, with much hesitation, started up the long steps, rang the bell at the front door and asked to see the Mother Superior. Before she arrived I could hear much whispering about me. When she came to the door, she wanted to know what I wanted. I told her I wanted to come in and visit with some of the old people because they looked lonely.

"Does your Mother know you are here?" she asked.

"No, Sister, but she won't mind," I fibbed. In all reality Mother would have been very upset with me. I did not realize that I shouldn't have gone without telling Mother where I was.

I remember talking for a few minutes to some ladies on the porch. Then chimes started ringing and a nun informed us it was time to go to the chapel for Mass. I helped push some of the wheelchairs to the chapel, and I sat down. After a few minutes I whispered to one of the nuns, "I have to go, I don't want my mother to worry if I am late."

I left and never went back. I don't know why!

CHAPTER 15

PASSION PLAY

While I was recuperating from the near-death experience I told you about in Chapter 12, our family would go to the country club to which we belonged. While Pete and our girls swam in the creek, I would sit on the dock with my Bible and a tablet. I was writing a Passion Play about Jesus' trial, crucifixion and his Ascension. I cannot remember when the thought came to me to do this. I can never remember thinking to myself, *Gee, this will be fun or nice to do.* I only found myself engrossed in my project. Perhaps when God allowed me to remain with my family on this earth, maybe he gave me an assignment that I could not recall. My subconscious mind just took over. After all the life-saving medication I had been given, there were periods of momentary memory loss and confusion.

When I finally finished the play, I wondered what to do with it. I was obsessed with finding a place to have it performed. I fantasized what a wonderful thing it would be if the whole city participated, maybe including several churches, and it could be held in the football stadium. I approached a large Baptist church and explained my ideas. "No thanks; it wouldn't work," I was told.

My cousin Mark had stopped by my house to find out what the people at the church had said. We were sitting at the dining room table hashing it over. He told me that if I could find a place, he would help me. At that point, I was so discouraged, I slapped the table with my hand and emphatically stated: "I will do this play somewhere . . . I have to."

About that time the script and all of my sketches started

blowing off the table. "Where in the world did that wind come from?" laughed Mark.

I jumped up and ran to the den to shut the glass sliding door. On my way back to the dining room, I almost tripped over a box of my kindergarten art work. As I glanced down, in the box there was a big five-point yellow star on a stick the children had used in a Christmas nativity play. I stopped abruptly, picked it up and stared at it. Approaching the table once again, I told Mark, "Maybe we can do this with my kindergarten children for the church where I work."

Very excited the next day, I approached the minister. "Sounds good to me," he said encouragingly. We agreed that we would have the play at the Wednesday Night Prayer Service before Easter Sunday.

Now we had four little children in my class who were from a boys' home. One of these children was withdrawn and would not do anything. He would not have conversation, work, color, or play. He didn't want to communicate with anybody. He just sat around quietly and listened. His name was Matthew, and he was a beautiful child, but quiet and sad.

One morning, after much thought, Wanda, the other teacher, and I decided we might be able to help Matthew if he would be in our play. So I sat in a little chair and called him to come over. "Matthew, would you like to be in our play?"

He said nothing, so I continued, "You don't have to if you don't want to, but we would like for you to play the part of Jesus, would you like to?"

He looked at me for a minute and asked, "Do I have to tell you now?"

"Well-l-l when do you think you can let me know?"

"Twenty minutes," he replied.

"Okay," I said, a bit puzzled.

He got out his rest mat, put it on the floor and lay down to think. Wanda and I were anxious to get started practicing the program, so in a few minutes I went to the mat and said, "Matthew, did you make your decision?"

"Has it been twenty minutes?"

"Well, not really," I answered honestly.

"Come back when the twenty minutes is over," he said in a little louder voice. Wanda and I sat in our little chairs waiting impatiently.

"Time's up," I informed him, ten minutes later.

He got up very slowly, folded his little mat and put it away. Then he walked right up to my face and quietly said, "I'll do it."

"Now, you do know that if you are going to have this special part you will have to start doing your work, sing and play like everybody else, Okay?" I said.

"Okay," he replied as he walked away. That started a wonderful reversal in his behavior. He was more relaxed and even smiled sometimes.

One morning we were preparing to have our daily snack of juice and cookies. I would always say a little prayer, like "Dear Lord, thank you for this beautiful day and for all my friends and my food. Amen." Then I would say, "Does anyone else want to talk to God?'"

Most of the time several little hands would go up and as I called upon the children one at a time, they would, out loud, talk to God and thank Him for their dog, frogs, rocks and their other prized possessions. Matthew never did. However, this particular morning as I glanced around the room asking, "Does anyone else want to talk to God?" I was thrilled when Matthew raised his little hand. After calling his name I closed my eyes, but as he was saying his prayer I opened my eyes to look at him and was stunned to see a brilliant yellow five-point star floating just above the child's head. I could hardly speak I was so overcome with shock. When the child said "Amen," the star disappeared.

Wanda had not been in the room at that time, but she came running out of the small choir storage room as pale as a ghost. She was terrified and was saying, "You'll never believe what happened to me!"

"Me too," I stuttered.

We hurried to wind up the day and get the children into their cars to go home. Then we sat down, and I told her about the star over Matthew's head. Then she told me that while this was happening to Matthew she was looking through a file cabinet in the choir storage room, and she could feel someone in the room standing behind her. She could feel them breathing on the back of her neck. When she turned, no one was there, but she said she could feel the presence. She was so terrified she almost passed out. Because of the layout of the choir storage room, we know no one was there! We were afraid to be in the building alone. The minister had gone home to lunch, but we had to tell somebody, so we called and pleaded with him to come back in a hurry. We were also afraid that he would think we were nuts and fire us or something.

When he arrived, we were trembling so much that we could barely talk. He listened so patiently and then he explained. The star was God blessing the child, and to confirm that this was a true spiritual happening, the Holy Spirit let its presence be known. If the star had appeared without the presence of being felt, it would not have any meaning. Wanda feeling the presence of the Holy Spirit as I was seeing the star, was the confirmation needed to let us know it was *all from God*, and God was pleased.

The children were very good as we practiced the play. Mark came and helped with the simple scenery.

The night of the presentation was wonderful. Matthew's part was moving, especially on the cross at the end. The spectators were overwhelmed with emotion; many were crying. At the end of the program, after the children had left the church to go back to the kindergarten room, seven people walked up the aisle to the minister and joined the church.

One morning, about six weeks later, Matthew and his house mother came to school. She smiled as she told me that the home had Awards Day and that Matthew had won the $10.00 award for being the most self-improved child!

All this happened several years ago, and I retired from that church kindergarten due to my daughter's and father-in-law's illnesses. Now I am back to work in a large Catholic church school. My dear friend, Nella, and I have presented my play twice, and each time it gets bigger and has more meaning. I plan to contact my friends Norman and Doris from Hardeville, and maybe we can take the play to their little church over there.

CHAPTER 16

MY BIG BROTHER LEON

My big brother Leon is only three years older than I, so as children we were very close companions. We played together all the time, and as we grew older, we were still very companionable. I thought he was the greatest brother in the whole world, and all my girlfriends, especially Ann Davis, thought he was "super." He was always looking out for me by screening my beaus and coaxing Mom to let me go places with the crowd. In return I'd lend him half of my allowance. The admiration and love for him was so great that it still holds a wonderful bond between us. Perhaps it is because of this bond that I find myself, as one might say, tuned into his brain waves. When he is upset, depressed or scared he is like a transmitter and I am his receiver.

I do believe we were together in another life. As a little girl,

I remember many nights after Mother and Daddy had gone to bed, I would get out of bed and tiptoe to see if Leon was home. If he was in his bed, I'd think, "Good," and go back to sleep. But any night he had gone out to a meeting or with friends and was late, I would sit in the dark living room, watching through the window, waiting for him. I'd cry, thinking maybe he wouldn't come home. When I saw him walking down the sidewalk, I would be so happy I would sob harder and run to my bed and jump under the covers so he wouldn't know I was still awake.

Leon always belonged to regimented clubs or organizations. In school it was the Boys Service Patrol, then the Boy Scouts. When World War II broke out, he was an Air Raid Warden for our neighborhood. As a teenager he went to Benedictene Military School, and as soon as he was old enough, he joined the Seabees.

Then he joined the Army and was soon in the Special Forces. I called it the Cloak and Dagger Squad. He was so happy and proud of his uniform, and he was dedicated to his country. You might say he gave his life to his county.

In 1950 he was in Korea. One night as I was lying in bed trying to go to sleep, I heard a very loud noise. It sounded as if a gun had gone off, but no one in the house had heard it but me. Instantly Leon's face flashed across my mind's eye. I knew immediately that he was hurt. I jumped out of bed and rushed over to my jewelry box and found the wings he had given to me when I was ill. I pinned his wings on my gown and held on to them as my thoughts went to Korea and Leon.

A week later a letter arrived from Leon to Mother telling her that he had been wounded but had asked that the family not be notified. It was his option to write and tell us.

A few weeks later I went to my car to retrieve a package that I had forgotten to bring inside. As I slipped across the seat I heard on the radio: "American planes are on standby red-alert loaded with hydrogen bombs." I was so upset I raced into the house. "Turn on the radio, quick; there has been a red alert in

Korea!" I screamed.

"What station?" inquired Pete.

"I don't know I heard it on the car radio" I answered.

Pete ran out to the car. The radio was not on.

"Why did you turn the radio off?" he asked. "I didn't touch it, it just came on by itself." I told him.

He hurriedly called several radio stations to find out about the announcement. Each one of them said the same thing" "There has been no such bulletins."

My friend, Betty, had come by and saw that I was visibly shaken. She went with me to our Catholic church where I lit a candle and prayed for God to protect Leon.

When I came home that afternoon, I made a tape. Instead of writing we made audio tapes to send to each other. In my tape I told him how worried I was and what I had heard on the radio. About two weeks later I got a tape back. It said, "Baby, you were very accurate in what you heard. But how in the hell could you know that? Don't put things like that on tapes as you will get me in trouble. Who in this man's army would believe that you were *reading me*?"

After that tour of duty, when he was back in the United States in Oklahoma, I received a telephone call from him. "We're having a party and, I have been telling my friends about you being my receiver. Could you go sit in the blue chair in your living room at exactly 10 p.m.? I am going to think something to you. Then we will call you back and you can tell them what it was. Okay?"

"Well, okay, but I don't know if it will work," I replied.

Promptly at the designated time I did as he asked. Relaxing and having a few minutes of quiet solitude, I just sat there and fixed a mental picture of Leon in my mind. I thought I heard his voice. Hardly believing this myself, I just sat there, spellbound. The sudden ringing of the telephone jolted me from my chair. It was his wife.

"What was he telling you?" she laughed.

I said quietly "This probably isn't right, but I think he was telling me something about his hair. Someone wants to dye his hair a stupid color."

She repeated what I had said to their guests, and I heard them laughing out loud. Then Bill, a friend of his took the telephone. "How did you do that?" he said, "How did you do that?"

Leon took the phone. "Baby, this crazy friend of mine has a wife who is a beautician, and he wants me to let her dye my hair purple for a parade that is on the base Saturday, which is to promote funds for a children's hospital. You came through 100%, honey; thanks, I'll think something to you again sometime soon. Bye!"

Unfortunately, Leon had several failed marriages . . . too much dedication to his military career and the inability to settle down, I guess. However, his first marriage gave him three wonderful sons. He loved the excitement of the Special Forces, and my daughters looked upon him as a James Bond figure.

On the evening of August 4, 1964, we had just retired when I heard a terrific explosion. Instantaneously a vision of a military vehicle flashed into focus, and Leon's name raced through my mind. A helicopter was broken in half, the front half being completely separated from the back section. There was no one in the helicopter or anywhere near it.

Very frightened, I jerked myself upright in bed and shook Pete. "What was that?"

"What was what?" he replied.

"That explosion."

"Well, I didn't hear anything," he sighed. "You were dreaming."

"No, I didn't dream it, I heard it with my ears," I insisted, as I explained about the vision that accompanied the sound. I did not sleep very well at all that night. Leon was on a tour of duty in Vietnam, and I felt as though some terrible accident had befallen him, and suddenly I began to cry. I just knew he was hurt or dead. All the next day I was very nervous, jumpy and very anxious. This was not my normal behavior. Anytime I went out of the house I would leave word where I could be located in case the family needed me in a hurry.

I was so worried that I went to the Cathedral to light a candle, say my prayers and ask God's mercy for my brother. As I was leaving, I noticed a very large statue of Christ lying in the arms of his precious mother Mary after his dead body had been taken down off the cross. As I looked at, this I thought, "What a beautiful piece of art." Then, as my eyes fell upon Mary's face, I noticed that in one of her eyes was a tear. Just one, lone single tear. At that moment, an indescribable feeling came over me. I knew this was just a statue, but as I looked at her tear, for the first time in my life I realized what she must have suffered as she watched her precious son die. Such agony I had in my heart, too, not knowing if my brother was injured or if he was lying helplessly somewhere, dying. I felt so much compassion for Mary that I broke into tears because never before had I ever thought of her emotion in her hour of grief.

Thirty-six miserable hours later we received word that on the fourth of August, at approximately the same time I had had this traumatic experience, Leon, a sergeant in the U.S. Army, had been injured in Vietnam. The helicopter he had been occupying had been shot down, but landed safely. Then the helicopter slid down a slope, and the tip of the ski touched off a land mine. No one was killed because the explosion had blown the helicopter in half and had thrown out all the men. They were all seriously injured but all survived. I was so thankful, for God had truly been merciful.

I wrote a book about Leon when he was overseas. It was about all the things we did when we were children. I named it *My Big Brother Leon*. I mailed it to him. I hope to publish it someday.

We mailed him boxes all the time. Once I sent him a birthday party package, with instructions to go get a friend to share his surprise. They were to put on the birthday hats, and there were candles for his cupcake, an 8-mm movie of all the family singing *Happy Birthday*. It was fun, and we always tried to do things to make him happy.

When he was in the "boondocks" in Vietnam I sent him, as a joke, a letter written in Braille. All one could see on the paper was little bumps. He was upset; he was afraid somebody would think I was sending him coded messages. He was always surprised when he received packages from me.

When he was coming home from Vietnam, I sent him a small box. Before he opened the well-taped box, a note read, "Hurry home, thousands await you." When he opened the box he found two dead mosquitoes. When I received a tape from him, he was laughing so hard he could hardly talk. But that was always my purpose, to keep his spirits up.

I told him, "Leon, if you ever become a prisoner of war, and they lock you up, then one day you might hear high heel shoes clinking down the hall and you will know I have come to get you out."

He would laugh and say "Okay!"

Because he was in the Army Intelligence many times he worked "under cover," appearing as a civilian. On one occasion he was assigned to an embassy in Austria. I was so relieved that he was no longer in the Vietnam war zone. I didn't have to worry about him being in danger.

Drifting off to sleep one night, I saw two men in shadow form struggling in a wrestling sort of way. One was severely beating the other. Soon, one dropped out of sight and to the ground. The other ran off, and the limp figure lay lifeless on the ground. I frantically sat up and told Pete, "Honey, Honey its Leon. He has been hurt again; he's hurt bad: somebody has beaten him up."

I jumped out of bed, grabbed a pen and some paper and wrote:

Dear Leon,

Tonight I had a terrible vision. If you have been hurt let us know.
Don't try to keep it from us because I know you have been injured
tonight. Answer this note soon to relieve my mind.

Love, Mildred

Ten anxious days later I received a reply:
Dear Babe:
I'll be damned if I can keep anything from you. Yes, on the night you discussed I was attacked by an intruder. As I entered my hotel room   the burglar had a lead pipe and beat me down to the floor. In the scuffle the other sleeping guests in the hotel were aroused, and it scared the man away. The doctor said it was a miracle I am alive. But here I am.
    Love, LEON

Later Leon told us the intruder was caught. He was another U.S. Army solider. He had taken my brother's tiny spy camera. He served time in jail and was dishonorably discharged.

One summer Pete and I were visiting Leon in Oklahoma. We had gone to the Officer's Club to dance and have some fun. We were sitting at the table when this Navy nurse, who was very crippled, and her husband walked up. She hugged and kissed Leon. They were so happy to see each other. When the men all went to the bar to get drinks, the nurse said, "Do you know why I am here today? It's because when we were in Korea your brother was the officer in command. I was seriously wounded. We had no vehicles to get back to camp, and it was snowing. Wounded men were everywhere. Lt. Martin carried me on his back and in his arms for thirty-six miles in the freezing snow. I love him. I owe him my life. Some of the men would fall and want to die, and he would jerk them up and order them to walk. You don't die when I'm in charge! They all got back. Frostbitten and near death but alive."

I know this has nothing to do with the supernatural purposes of this book, but I want the world to know he was a *good man.*

Leon retired after twenty-six years in the Army. It was very hard for him to settle down. He was bored most of the time and easily excitable. Unfortunately, he turned to alcohol to escape his depression. He often mentioned things that he had to do that totally bothered him.

While he had been in Vietnam he was a member of a group of men called "McCarthy Raiders." These men were especially chosen for their highly classified clearance and skills. Once Captain McCarthy had asked for volunteers to go on a special mission upon which the possibility of no return was great. Leon volunteered because the other raiders had small children, and his were grown. So Leon and several others went on the raid. When they returned safely, they found their camp had been hit by mortar and all the men had been killed. He had a very difficult time getting over that tragedy.

The family had hoped that he would be able to pull himself back together after he was home awhile.

One evening I was in a grocery store when I heard a man crying. I looked around and didn't see anyone. *That's Leon,* I thought.

I hurried over to his apartment to find him devastated and in tears. "What in the world is the matter? I thought it was you I heard crying." I had never seen my brother cry.

"I just got word that Captain McCarthy was killed," he said. "How did you know I was upset?" he asked, wiping his eyes.

"Well, would you believe I was in the grocery store to buy some coffee and bread when my inner ears heard you?" We both laughed, and then he felt better.

Since Leon had sustained so much trauma to his head, scar tissue had begun to grow and put pressure on his brain. This condition is what the doctors described as *organic brain syndrome.* Pressure eventually pressed on his brain that caused him not to be able to walk.

We had hired a friend of ours, Rosemary, to be his housekeeper. One day she called to tell me that some people had moved in with him. They were keeping him drugged and intoxicated so they could drive his car. They had even been cashing his checks and using the money. They had also taken his guns. Rosemary was very upset and said, "Please come and make them leave."

I went every day but never could catch them there. Early in the morning, mid-day, early evening, even late at night but I never could find them. This went on for about two weeks and the family was worried to death.

Then, one dreary, rainy night, we had company. We were all sitting in my living room, visiting. Pete had turned on the television and we were all watching *The Lawrence Welk Show*. The music was beautiful. I leaned my head against the back of my chair and closed my eyes. After a minute, in my mind's eye, my deceased father suddenly appeared in the living room. His appearance was as much younger man than when he had died. He walked very quickly across the living room to the front door and grasped the knob very firmly. Then he disappeared. It frightened me badly. I realized he was telling me to go out the door for some reason, but where? In a second or two the realization hit me. "Oh God, I know what I have got to do," I stammered as I jumped up from my chair, grabbed my raincoat and keys and ran out the door to my car.

My family thought I had gone nuts. "Where are you going in this storm?" Pete yelled after me.

"To Leon's house, Daddy is trying to tell me I can catch them if I hurry," I hollered.

Thanking my father for watching over us from the other side, I walked into Leon's house, confronted the woman and her companion, ordered them to be out by the next morning or I would call the police. It worked! I still have to laugh when I think of myself, a small-framed five-foot-two woman, looking up to the approximately six-foot-three, two-hundred pounder and ordering her around. Reminds me of Mutt and Jeff. I was so angry at her I never stopped to think she could have shot me or knocked me out.

Shortly after this we took Leon to the Charleston Veterans Hospital. They helped to get him into the Chatham Nursing Home, and the family appointed me as his guardian.

It took a while, but he finally got adjusted to the nursing home and his wheelchair, thanks to some very special ladies he met at the nursing home. The head nurse, Carey Tidwell, was a wonderful help to his adjustment. She understood and respected his emotions, depressions and frustrations. Then Ruby LaCombe, the supervisor of housekeeping, grew to be a very dear and loving friend.

After he had been there six years, he developed lung cancer. What a battle that was. He was brave for me and I was being brave for him, but it was eating both our hearts out. Near the end I hired sitters for night time, as he didn't want to be alone.

About two o'clock one morning the sitter called. "Your brother wants to know if you can come and be with him for awhile?"

"Tell him I am on the way," I said. This was several days before he died.

I was rolling him up and down the quiet halls in his wheelchair while everybody else was asleep except the nurses' aides. He suddenly broke down, crying uncontrollably. Putting my arms around him and hugging him (I needed to cry but tried to control myself), he looked into my eyes and sobbed, "Did you ever see a flower growing out of somebody's eye? I did! A young soldier in Vietnam who we came across had a tiny flower growing out of his eye."

I could not say anything, trying to hold back my tears, to be strong for him.

A nurses' aide came over and said, "Sgt. Martin, lets say a prayer together." She took our hands and prayed. He smiled!

My God, no wonder he drank trying to forget all the atrocities he had seen in his twenty-six year military career, I thought as I rolled him back to his room and he got into bed.

"Please just hold my hand until I go to sleep," he cried. I hugged him and kissed him and, holding his hand, sat quietly by his bed until he fell asleep. I cried all the way home.

On April 18, 1988, he passed into the next world.

CHAPTER 17

CASSADAGA HERE I COME

Leon had been ill for so long, and, being the big brother, he had always been my strength. I knew he was being the soldier and was holding up for so me I wouldn't go to pieces on him. Because our mother was also a patient in the nursing home, she was with us every day. I didn't want her to know anything was wrong. I had disciplined myself so intensely that when Leon died I could never seem to let go of my emotions. Maybe that was my denial. I just didn't want to let go because I didn't want to accept his being gone. About a month after the funeral I had gone to bed rather late, and I was very depressed.

In a dream Leon came to me. He walked to my bedroom door and just stood there. He was in his full-dress uniform, and he looked so very handsome. I got out of bed and ran over to him.

"Leon its you," I sobbed.

He put his arms around me, and we hugged and I cried. As he held me in his arms, he said, "Baby, don't cry; we will always be together; I promise, and remember I love you."

I was hugging him so tight and I said, "I love you too."

Then he was gone, and I woke up crying and could not stop crying for three days. It was so strange to think that it took my big brother Leon coming back from the grave to console me. No one in the world could convince me he was not there that night. I could feel his arms and body. Spirit? Okay, yes . . . but he was with me!

Ann, our sister, lives in Florida near Cassadaga, the spiritualist center of the South. I like to go there sometimes. It's fun to have a reading from a psychic or medium. It can get a little "spooky" with all the old houses and quaint little hilly streets.

Years ago I had my first reading. The lady who performed the reading knew nothing about me, but she told me a spirit was there with me and that her name started with an "R." I knew immediately that it was Aunt Ruth.

A visit to a different medium was very interesting. She asked me if I had three daughters. When I confirmed that I did, she said, "You and your oldest daughter were together in another life; you were sisters. I can see you sitting together in a corner of a dark room, hugging each other. You are crying because your mother is dead. Your father is a sea captain and only comes home once in a while. A nanny takes care of you." What is so strange about this is that I had painted a picture of an old Spanish Galleon, all broken up in rough water.

I am scared to death of water, so why I would choose to paint a ship I do not know. Maybe it was a flashback of some kind from another life. I remember seeing a picture in a *National Geographic* of a large ship that was sinking, and instantly I wanted to paint a picture of it. By the way, I sold it to the Ships of the Sea Museum.

Another medium told me that a man I cared for would soon pass away and that the numbers 8 and 6 had something to do with it. A year later Leon passed away on the 18th of April, 1988, at 6 p.m. His room number was 216. I thought it very unusual the numbers of 6 and 8 were repeated.

A few months before Leon died he expressed the desire to go see Ann in Florida. I really felt like he wouldn't be able to go, but to keep his spirits up, I told him when he got a little stronger we would drive down to see her. Of course, we never got to make the trip, at least when he was alive.

A workshop was being offered in Past Life Regression by Ron DeVasto, and I really wanted to attend, but I didn't want to go alone.

My nephew, Donnie, lives in Orlando, so I invited his wife, Kathy, to go with me. We were a little apprehensive about going but had fun. There were approximately thirty-five people there.

In the first half of our session we were taught how to relax and position our bodies so that we could be responsive to the hypnotic state we were preparing to enter. As we sat there, eyes closed, feet flat on the floor, hands in our laps, palms up, the psychic started the audio tape.

The music was beautiful, and as I listened, the weight of my body seemed to sink into the chair. Suddenly tears streamed down my right eye — only my right eye. I could not seem to move my arm and hand to wipe the tears off my cheek. In wonderment, I gave in and just let the tears flow freely. I wasn't sad! What was happening? I felt so peaceful!

About that time the audio tape had concluded, and we were supposed to open our eyes and return to our natural selves.

I told Kathy about the tears, and she reminded me immediately in an excited voice that some of Leon's head injuries he sustained in Vietnam and Austria had damaged his left eye. He had made a statement some time ago that every time he had a cold, his right eye would run water, but never his left, due to the damage of the optic nerves.

Then our instructor asked if anyone had any questions or was concerned with anything they had experienced. I raised my hand slowly and bashfully. When I was acknowledged I explained about the tears, the inability to wipe them away, the heaviness my body experienced and the inner peace within myself.

He scared me when he stated, "If you want to know I will tell you, but I do not want to frighten you. If anyone here wants to leave before I explain this situation, feel free to go. I do not want to upset anyone." He paused for a moment; no one left.

He looked at me and said, "Do you know anyone recently deceased that had problems with their eyes?"

"Yes, my brother he passed away this April," I trembled.

"You loved him very much?"

"That's right, we were very close," I quivered.

"Well, his entity entered your body, but you are okay now, right?"

"Yes."

"Well he just wanted to let you know he is with you. So do not be afraid; he will never harm you."

Kathy and I got up and went outside in complete disbelief. We had lunch and walked around. We even sat down at the old cemetery and read some of the tombstones of the deceased psychics and mediums and walked down to Lake Colby.

The time came to go back to the second half of our Past Life Regression workshop. As we went in, we had to sign a paper stating we would hold no one responsible for any adverse reactions while under the hypnotic state.

In this part of our workshop we were supposed to be taken back in time to another life. I thought if this worked I would find myself working in an orphanage, living on a farm, maybe married to a minister or be an artist or musician. However, I was very skeptical that I would see anything. Was I surprised!

The assembly quieted down quickly; the lights dimmed, and we sat as we had been instructed earlier. An audio tape began playing. The music was very soothing and relaxing. As I sat there, my eyes closed. Ron took us on a mind's journey to a lake and a walk along a beach. We could visualize dolphins playing in the water. Then he led us back up the sandy beach, when suddenly he said, "Stop, look behind you! You see yourself in another life, another time, another place."

In utter amazement a woman appeared in my mind's eye. She had long, black, silky hair. She wore a tan-colored very plain dress. It resembled the kind of attire an Indian or Mexican peasant would wear. (See Vision I)

Then our instructor asked, "Are you alone, or is someone with you?" Instantly in my vision a man appeared standing next to the woman. He was of average height and slim, but he had a

Past Lives

Vision I

Indian or Mexican
woman, black hair.
Simple peasant
dress. Bare feet.
House like a box, made of some clay
material, a flat roof with large poles at roof.

Vision II

Indian or Mexican man
Peasant clothes - white
full shirt with
blousey sleeves.
Dark pants. Standing
by house. He is not
chubby, but real full face

Vision III   Death Scene

man kneeling beside
her, praying.
She is lying on
a cot made
of some canvas
Type material, with wood legs.

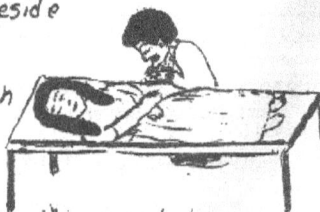

very, very muscular chest, olive skin, jet black hair and moustache. He was dressed in black tight pants and a white shirt with bloused sleeves. (See Vision II)

Next, Ron said, "Where are you? Are you inside a building or outside?" Immediately a house came into focus; it was like a box. It looked as if it were made of clay material. It had a flat roof, but I could see several large poles at the roof top. The door was made of old rough-looking wood. The house was standing on barren land, no trees, grass or vegetation. The land looked hard and baked.

The last instruction was to "Go forward to the time of your death. Are you alone?" he asked.

Into my vision flashed a woman lying on a cot, her arms folded across her chest as if she was dead. The same man was kneeling beside her, his arms resting on the side of the cot, hands clasped together, head bowed as if he were praying over her. (See Vision III)

Then we were brought back to the present simply by the suggestion to return back to our present life. In a few minutes we were told to open our eyes but to remember what we had experienced.

The session ended. Kathy and I were bewildered. However, Kathy laughed as she confessed that she had been so tired she had fallen asleep.

When we left Cassadega, Kathy went back to Orlando, and I jumped in my car and drove to Daytona Beach, where Ann and Jack had rented a condominium on the beach for a month.

When I got to their place, I found them sitting in the living room.

"How did it go?" Ann inquired.

"You will never believe it," I replied.

"Come sit on the sofa and tell us about it," Jack said, as he handed me a cool glass of wine.

"Do you remember me telling you that Leon had wanted me to bring him down here before he died?" I asked. "Well, he is here with me now."   They all laughed as I began telling them my story.

"Ah-h-h now," Jack laughed. Just as that remark came out of his mouth the light behind the sofa where I was sitting started to blink off-and-on, off-and-on, off-and-on.

"Listen," said Ann in a joking way, "you go sit over in that chair across the room; don't sit next to me." We all giggled as I moved to the other chair.

I continued my explanation of the workshop, and as I was telling about the tears rolling down my cheek, the lamp next to my chair also started blinking off-on, off-on. "I told you he had come with me."

"Leon, we love you but you are scaring us." Ann trembled.

Kathy called my house in Savannah when returned from our trip. She told me her bathroom light was also blinking. They had it checked out, but there was nothing wrong. We decided that Leon had gone to their house too. He stayed with them several days, blinking their light.

About a year ago I attended another workshop. The instructor, Mrs. Miskelly, had the group in a huge circle. Quickly and quietly everyone in the group became relaxed and began meditating. She was teaching us how to open our minds to our spirit guides. Our eyes closed, hands palms up, the backs of our hands resting in our laps, we became aware of soft beautiful music playing.

Suddenly in my relaxed state, I was aware that my legs felt too heavy to move. My right hand felt heavy, as though I was holding something in it. I could bend the fingers of my left hand but not my right. What was in my hand? What a strange sensation.

My mind began pondering over the unusual sensations and instantaneously my right eye began running tears again, and I realized what was going on. Leon, my brother and spirit guide, was with my again.

When all the lights were back on, Mrs. Miskelly asked if anyone experienced any special feelings they would like to share. I raised my hand shyly. I spoke out to the assembly and explained about my legs not wanting to move and the weight in my right hand, also about my tears. Then I said, "My brother lives in the spirit world. Before he passed away I took care of him. He could not walk and a few minutes ago I couldn't move my legs. When he would feel so much pain from his cancer he would yell, "Baby," and quickly reach out for my hand. We would hold hands until the pain passed. I knew it was Leon's hand I was holding just now when the tears started flowing from my right eye, just as he cried only from one eye. I feel my brother is here with me today. He wants me to know he is happy that I am still tuned in to him."

I left the workshop with very mixed emotions — happy to have experienced such a beautiful reunion and yet sad not to be able to see my brother.

CHAPTER 18

THE END OR THE BEGINNING

Leon had been a Shriner for years. He was an active member of the Alee Temple Carnival Unit (for children). He could not walk, but he could operate the tiny Ferris wheel from his wheelchair.

Once a year the Shriners had a memorial service for all the deceased members of their lodge.

Since I had been Leon's legal guardian, I was invited to attend as his representative. Dickie, his youngest son, went also. I took Leon's Bible and picture with me. I kept the picture in the Bible so no one would see it. I felt that if I could take a peep at him once in awhile, I would feel like he was there with Dickie and me.

It was a beautiful service. They had a big floral wreath (a broken wheel) with no flowers on it. Each representative was given a Carnation and instructed that when the name was called of the deceased Shriner he or she represented, we were supposed to walk down to the wreath and insert our flower. Dickie was shy and didn't want to do it, so I did.

Soon the wreath was completely filled, and it was beautiful. There were many tears in the audience. I was very glad Dickie and I had been there.

The next day I went to the Chatham Nursing Home to tend to my mother. I was standing by the sink combing mother's hair when I saw Ruby LaCombe walking down the hall. When I waved at her, she came into Mother's room and gave us a hug. She was fond of Leon and our entire family.

In great detail I began telling her about the Shriners'

ceremony. She said, "I wish you had let me know; I would have like to have gone with you and Dickie. I loved Leon, you know."

At that moment, a nurse's aide bolted into the room. "What's the matter?" she said in a panicky voice.

"What do you mean?" asked Ruby.

"Well, I was at the nurse's station, and all of a sudden Mrs. Martin's bell started going nuts, like there was some kind of an emergency," the aide reported.

"Nobody rang the bell. We haven't even been near her bed. The three of us have been here by the sink talking for the past fifteen minutes," I stated flatly.

"Well don't tell me I am wrong because her bell was almost ringing off the wall," the very disgusted aide stated as she turned abruptly and marched out of the room.

Ruby and I looked at each other and at the same time said, "It's Leon — he did it — he is here."

"He heard us talking about him and wanted us to know that he was here with us, and he was probably at the Alee Temple with you Sunday," injected Ruby.

Our eyes searched the room questioningly hoping for another sign of his presence. But our hearts knew! Ruby and I both wiped our tears, and after another hug, she went on back to her office.

Leon, among other things, was an electronic expert. He would know how to do such a thing. Besides, spirits use vibrations and energy to maneuver.

Michael, my little five-year-old grandson, was outside in the backyard playing in the dirt, digging with a big spoon.

I was watching him out of my kitchen window. He looked so cute and was content. I knocked on the window really hard with my knuckles. He looked up at me questioningly. I waved and smiled, and he waved and smiled back. When he came into the kitchen a few minutes later I said, "Michael, do you know what I was telling you when I knocked on the window?"

"Yes, ma'am; you were telling me that you loved me," he answered with a grin.

"That's right, honey, I was saying that I loved you."

That night I was sitting in the den writing in my book when I realized it was eleven o'clock. *No wonder I'm so tired, I had better put this up and go to bed.* I turned off the television set and most of the lights; then I strolled into the kitchen thinking I might like a glass of milk. As I was standing quietly by the refrigerator trying to decide if I really wanted the milk, something knocked very loudly three times on my kitchen window. I was terrified! I raced to the bedroom and, shaking Pete from a deep sleep, I screamed, "Wake up, wake up somebody is in the yard. They knocked on the window at me."

Pete jumped out of bed, got his gun and flashlight. He quietly opened the sliding glass door and, searching the perimeter with his flashlight, moved slowly to the yard,

He returned to the house in a minute. "Look how high the window is off the ground. Nobody could reach that high to knock on it." Then he turned the flashlight on our two big dogs who were lying fast asleep near their dog house. "Look at the dogs. If anyone was in this yard they would be raising Cain. Come on to bed, it was just your imagination."

"Listen something did knock on that window, I don't care what you say; I heard it loud and clear."

Pete patted me on my shoulder and strolled back to bed, shaking his head in a negative manner. I stood in the kitchen once again, alone and bewildered, trying to interpret this puzzle. Suddenly there was a flashback to that morning and my conversation with Michael. *Knocking on the window meant I love you.* Oh, God, Leon is here telling me that he loves me. He must have heard our conversation this morning. When he died I thought this was the end of our being able to communicate, but maybe it's not the end . . . just a new beginning in our relationship. This is the way of the spirit world. I stood there in tears, talking to an empty kitchen, telling Leon how much I loved him and missed him. Then I went to bed.

About a week after that episode, there had been a big dance on Saturday evening at the hotel at which Kathleen works. On Monday she called and told us there were a lot of helium-filled balloons left over from the dance, and if I wanted some, I could come get them because the room had to be emptied and the balloons would have to be thrown away. So the children and I went down to the hotel and loaded the car with large black and white balloons.

When we returned to my house, the balloons got scattered. So we decided to take some outside and release them into the atmosphere. Little Michael asked if he could hold one. When I gave it to him, he said, "Wait a minute," then disappeared into the library. In a few minutes he reappeared, and I could tell he had something in his hand that he did not want us to see. He was trying to attach this small paper to the balloon string.

When I asked what was on the paper, he didn't want to tell me. Thinking it was probably a silly note with our telephone number or something. I insisted, "Let me see what you wrote on the paper or throw it away."

He very timidly opened it; it read:

UNCLE LEON
I miss you
I love you
I hope you feel better
    Love, Michael

I almost died! That precious child loved his uncle very, very much. He went with me often to see Leon at the nursing home. My brother would be sitting in his chair and say, "Hello, little man," and give him a lollipop.

"Will Uncle Leon get this note up in Heaven if I put it on my balloon?" he asked in a soft, tearful voice.

"Yes, honey, he will and it will make him so-o-o happy," I said, shaking my tears back once again.

As we went outside everybody watched as Michael released his balloon. "Here it is, Uncle Leon, catch it," he said quietly.

I prayed that God would allow that one very special balloon to rise up into Heaven so that the child could believe he had received his message. Up-up-up it went until it disappeared into the clouds.

Leon, wherever you are, we will be watching and waiting to hear form you. Maybe knock on my window sometime. Maybe someday you can even *think* something to me again.

The end . . . or the beginning?

CHAPTER 19

THE BEGINNING OF THE END

Chapter 18 ended with, "Is this the beginning or is it the End?" Would my psychic experiences keep happening or would they cease now that I had written it all down in black and white. It took a while, but the visions started to reappear. So I will continue now to share my strange happenings with you.

On the night of May 20, 1998, I was getting ready for bed when suddenly I felt an urgent need to rush back to the nursing home where my mother had lived for 12 years. Pete, my husband, exclaimed, "It's 9 o'clock and you know she was okay tonight when you put her to bed."

I told him I had to go. "I can almost hear her calling me, and I sense she needs me *now!*" I jumped in the car and hurried to the nursing home.

Upon arriving I quickly and quietly went to her room. There she lay, so beautiful and sweet. I walked over to her, took her hand, and said, "Mama, are you all right?"

She opened her precious little eyes and smiled a tiny smile. I was holding her hand and telling her how much I loved her and how I appreciated her when suddenly she coughed once and almost stopped breathing. I frantically rang the bell for the nurse and rushed to the door to shout for help. I quickly gathered Mother in my arms and held her as she passed away.

Now why tell all this? Because I had always prayed for God to let me be with my mother when she passed into the next world; I did not want her to be alone. So it had to be a message I received from my Guardian Angel compelling me, "Go now!"

CHAPTER 20

UNEXPECTED WEDDING GUEST

On December 4, 1999, my granddaughter Suzie was getting married to David Callaway, a fine young man. The wedding was in a tiny little church at Shellman's Bluff. Our family was busy preparing the church, and as we were decorating the social hall for the reception, we talked about my mom continuously. The children all called her "Grandmother Annie."

On the altar we used some beautiful green plants that had been sent to her funeral. For the reception we used many of Mother's crystal platters, bowls and candy dishes. As we all worked to get ready for the celebration we would laugh and talk about how Mother would have loved to have been here with us. The bride and groom even used a pair of Mother's beautiful antique crystal champagne goblets from which to drink their wedding toast.

Thomas, my son-in-law, was our photographer. He used his video camera to record the whole ceremony. He was a little upset as he told us that he had to turn off the camera for a second while David's grandmother was walking down the aisle because "green" had come into view across the lens of the camera.

About a week after the wedding, Thomas brought the tape of the wedding over to my house. As we watched it, we could see the green, sheer discoloration that had upset Thomas. We told him not to worry, and laughing said, "It was probably Grandmother Annie."

A few days later I was watching a show on TV about psychics. They were using high-tech machines to try to capture a glimpse of spirits or ghosts. Suddenly, an apparition appeared on the screen. It looked similar to a sheer drape floating in the air. Startled, I realized it greatly resembled the green, sheer-looking spot on the wedding tape. So I hurried to find the tape of the wedding. I fast forwarded it until I came across the green sheer-looking object on the tape. Shocked by this, I realized that the green object must be my mother's spirit. One fascinating thing about it is that it would have been my mother's turn to walk down the aisle. David's parents walked down the aisle first, his mother, and then the last female member of his family, his grandmother.

Now if my mother had been alive it would have been her turn next, and that is exactly where the green sheer-like object appeared. Amazed by all of this, I paused the tape and used a 35-mm camera to capture the spirit's picture so I could always have it to share. The next day, I took the film to be developed.

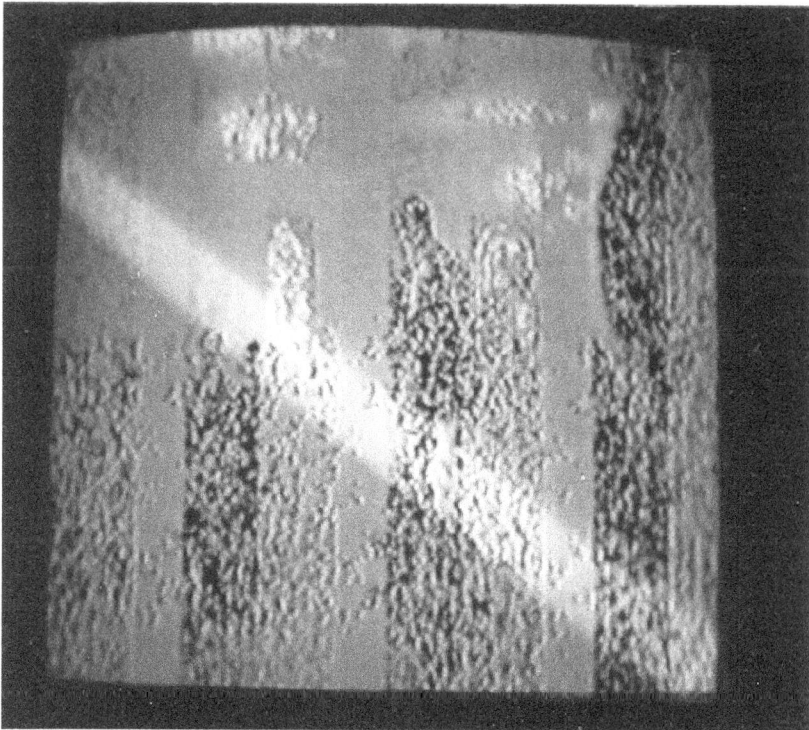

When the pictures finally came back, we were astonished. The transparent green object was there and through it you could clearly see one of the ushers. Then behind him were two faces — the tall one was my deceased brother Leon. He was escorting my mother's spirit down the aisle. My mother's face is not as clear as Leon's, but, after all, it was my mother's turn and she was determined to be there.

How miraculous it was to catch a spirit's picture on a photo. Thank you, God, for now I truly know they are still here with us and probably participate in most of our family functions.

CHAPTER 21

BIBLE SURPRISES

At the beautiful nursing home where my mother resided, there had begun to be some unsavory conditions that concerned me. I had been keeping records of how neglected most of the patients were due to the overworked nurses and aides. Each aide had too many patients to care for properly.

There was to be a county meeting at the nursing home and I was curious as to what mistruths would be told by the administrator to cover up the deficiencies. Some friends and acquaintances that also had family members in the nursing home also were concerned and wanted to go with me. We decided we would sit in the back of the meeting so we would not be noticed. Before the meeting started I was in my mother's room and saw that her Bible had been moved from her bedside table. As I picked it up I thought about my minister friend, Brother Arms.

Brother Arms once told me about a decision he had had to make concerning a church contract. Expecting a representative to come soon for his decision, he said he opened his Bible at random and the first words he saw were ". . . there was a knock on the door and three men appeared." As he put the Bible down there was a knock on his office door and as he opened it, there stood three men. Of course, he signed the contract.

Worried about the terrible situation at the nursing home, I opened my Bible for comfort. Opening it at random – the first words that I read were, "Lift up your voice o' Daughter and let it be heard" (Isaiah 1-30). Of course I was startled by the appropriateness of the message. Without hesitating, I stood up and as the Bible said, I "lifted up my voice and let it be heard!" Soon the administrator resigned and with a new director it has become, once again, a beautiful home for the elderly.

Several years later I was reminiscing with some old friends about the old days of World War II when so many strange or emotional things happened. I was telling them a story about when I was probably 10 years old. I was visiting a schoolmate that lived seven blocks from my home. It was very cold weather. Noticing the darkness approaching, I told my friend Jane I'd better leave so Mother would not be worried about me.

Across the street from her house was a motel. As I was leaving I noticed across the street on the porch of the motel were a soldier and his wife. They were standing in the cold holding a tiny baby wrapped in a blanket. The lady was crying. I was upset so I walked across the street and asked, "Ma'am, are you okay? Why are you crying?"

She replied, "They do not have a room and we don't know where we can spend the night." They did not have a car.

I said, "Lady, please don't cry, I know where you can stay. Just follow me."

The soldier asked, "Little girl, are you positive you know a place?" They hesitated to follow a small child, but in the end they did. It was really getting dark and very cold. We walked from 35th and Montgomery to my home at 513 West 38th street — seven long blocks.

When we got to my house, I told them to wait on the porch. I told my mother I'd brought a soldier, his wife, and their baby home to sleep. She almost fainted. But she called our neighbor next door, Mrs. Ola Johnson, who rented rooms. She was able to make room for them only because her daughter Lena was out of town. I walked them next door and gave Mrs. Johnson a big hug.

After they were all settled, I went home and cried. I told Mother, "When I saw them crying on that porch, all I could think about was Ann." My sister Ann was married to a soldier and it might have been her with no where to go out of the cold.

After relating this antiquated story to my old friends, they said, "And a little child shall lead them."

Wow! Suddenly I realized that was a Bible verse. So later I looked it up in the Bible out of curiosity and I could not believe my eyes. Can you believe the verse *"and a little child shall lead them"* is in Isaiah II-6 and is on the same page as the verse *"lift up your voice o' Daughter and let it be heard"*? What a miracle! How many pages are in a Bible? Fifteen hundred or more? Two separate happenings, 60 years apart and on the same page in the Bible. What can I say?

Incidentally the book of Isaiah is about a prophet. The text to which I refer is on page 122.

I was talking to Jared, my youngest 12-year-old grandson, about my psychic experience concerning the Bible. Jared asked "Do you think I could look in the Bible for a message?" I told him I didn't think it would work for him, because most anything he pointed to would not make any sense as far as a message goes. But he was pleading so seriously. Jared had been extremely ill for years and almost died. Finally, after finding the wonderful doctors in Jacksonville and many surgeries, he has regained much of his health.

"Okay, Jared, now take the Bible in your hands, close your eyes, and at random open it to any page. Very quickly point to and remember the first words you see in your message. It probably won't make sense, but give it a try."

So Jared did as instructed. The book he had opened to was II Samuel. He quickly pointed with one finger to the middle of the page, verse 33. We were astonished at the verse. It read, *"God is my strength and power and he maketh my way perfect."*

What a miracle! I am sure God himself guided his small, little finger to give him the message he needed. Because, for sure without God's help, he would not still be here on earth, but in Heaven.

"Thank you, God."

24 Therefore thus saith the Lord GOD of hosts, O my people that dwellest in Zion, be not afraid of the Assyrian: he shall smite thee with a rod, and shall lift up his staff against thee, after the manner of Egypt.

25 For yet a very little while, and the indignation shall cease, and mine anger in their destruction.

26 And the LORD of hosts shall stir up a scourge for him according to the slaughter of Midian at the rock of Oreb: and as his rod was upon the sea, so shall he lift it up after the manner of Egypt.

27 And it shall come to pass in that *day, that* his burden shall be taken away from off thy shoulder, and his yoke from off thy neck, and the yoke shall be destroyed because of the anointing.

The approach of the Gentile hosts to the battle of Armageddon (Rev. 16. 14; 19. 11).

28 He is come to Aiath, he is passed to Migron; at Michmash he hath laid up his carriages:

29 They are gone over the passage: they have taken up their lodging at Geba; Ramah is afraid; Gibeah of Saul is fled.

30 Lift up thy voice, O daughter of Gallim: cause it to be heard unto Laish, O poor Anathoth.

31 Madmenah is removed; the inhabitants of Gebim gather themselves to flee.

32 As yet shall he remain at Nob that day: he shall shake his hand against the mount of the daughter of Zion, the hill of Jerusalem.

33 Behold, the Lord, the LORD of hosts, shall lop the bough with terror: and the high ones of stature shall be hewn down, and the haughty shall be humbled.

Marginal references:

B.C. 713.

a Armageddon (battle of). vs.27-34; Isa.24.21-23. (Rev.16.14; 19.21.)

b Kingdom (O.T.). vs.1-12; Isa.24.23. (Gen.1.26; Zech.12.8.)

c Israel (prophecies). vs.1-13; Isa.60.1-12. (Gen.12.2,3; Rom.11.26.)

d Isa.4.2, note.

e Holy Spirit. Isa.32.15. (Gen.1.2; Mcl.2.15.)

f Psa.19.9, note.

g Psa.72.2,4; Rev.19.11.

h Righteousness (garment). Isa. 59.17. (Gen. 3.21; Rev. 19.8.)

i Isa.65.25; Ezk.34.25; Hos.2.18.

34 And he shall cut down the thickets of the forest with iron, and Lebanon shall fall by a mighty one.

CHAPTER 11.

[1] *The Davidic kingdom set up:* (1) *The King's ancestry.* (Cf. Mt. 1. 1.)

AND there shall [2]come forth a *b*rod out of the stem of *c*Jesse, and a *d*Branch shall grow out of his roots:

(2) *The source of the King's power: the sevenfold Spirit.* (Cf. Rev. 1. 4.)

2 And the *e*spirit of the LORD shall rest upon him, the spirit of wisdom and understanding, the spirit of counsel and might, the spirit of knowledge and of the *f*fear of the LORD;

(3) *The character of his reign.*

3 And shall make him of quick understanding in the *f*fear of the LORD; and he shall not judge after the sight of his eyes, neither reprove after the hearing of his ears:

4 But *g*with righteousness shall he judge the poor, and reprove with equity for the meek of the earth: and he shall smite the earth with the rod of his mouth, and with the breath of his lips shall he slay the wicked.

5 And righteousness shall be the *h*girdle of his loins, and faithfulness the girdle of his reins.

(4) *The quality of the kingdom.*

6 The *i*wolf also shall dwell with the lamb, and the leopard shall lie down with the kid; and the calf and the young lion and the fatling together; and a little child shall lead them.

7 And the cow and the bear shall feed; their young ones shall lie

---

[1] The *order of events* in Isa. 10., 11., is noteworthy. Isa. 10. gives the distress of the Remnant in Palestine in the great tribulation (Psa. 2. 5; Rev. 7. 14), and the approach and destruction of the Gentile hosts under the Beast (Dan. 7. 8; Rev. 19. 20). Isa. 11. immediately follows with its glorious picture of the kingdom-age. Precisely the same order is found in Rev. 19., 20. (See "Kingdom," O.T., Gen. 1. 26-28; Zech. 12. 8; N.T., Lk. 1. 31-33; 1 Cor. 15. 28. Also Mt. 3. 2, *note*; 6. 33, *note.*)

That nothing of this occurred at the first coming of Christ is evident from a comparison of the history of the times of Christ with this and all the other parallel prophecies. So far from regathering dispersed Israel and establishing peace in the earth, His crucifixion was soon followed (A.D. 70) by the destruction of Jerusalem, and the utter scattering of the Palestinian Jews amongst the nations.

[2] This chapter is a prophetic picture of the glory of the future kingdom. This is the kingdom announced by John Baptist as "at hand." It was then rejected, but will be set up when David's Son returns in glory (Lk. 1. 31, 32; Acts 15. 15, 16).

CHAPTER 22

VISIT FROM THE BLESSED MOTHER

Pete and I had owned a small piece of property on a creek; it was nice, but we never built anything on it. The time came when we needed to sell it because we needed the money for medical emergencies. We were discussing making a large "for sale" sign and putting it on the road.

On our back screen porch I had been painting a 4' x 8' picture of a Spanish dancer.

It was hanging on the wall of the porch. Jokingly, I said to Pete "we could put 'for sale' on the back of the Spanish lady's picture and let her face the creek." Then people riding up and down the creek could have a big laugh. Pete gave me a look of mild disgust.

Anxiously needing to get the "for sale" sign painted I hurried to my bedroom to put on my shoes. I plopped down on my bed to tie them. Sitting there I looked onto the porch through my sliding-glass door at the Spanish lady. Suddenly, I was stunned by what I saw. In a flash, the Spanish lady turned into the Blessed Mother. What a miraculous happening! She was there for a moment or two. Overwhelmed with excitement I started screaming uncontrollably and ran onto the porch to touch her. But the Blessed Mother vanished. I began sobbing with emotion while trying to explain to Pete what miracle had just transpired. He called our daughters to tell them. After I had calmed down I explained exactly what I had seen. The 4' x 8' board had turned from gray to blue and the Spanish lady had become a beautiful fair-skinned woman in white robes. There were gold stars all around her; the whole vision had become oval-shaped. Who would ever believe me?

That same afternoon I acquired a saw and some paint. I completely covered the whole 4' x 8' board in white. I then trimmed the board into an oval shape with the saw. Then as best I could, I outlined the form of the Blessed Mother and had her painted in two days.

We forgot all about making a for-sale sign. Never would I ever write on the back of where She had been. In a week or two we took the painting of the Blessed Mother to the creek and secured it under a beautiful oak tree overlooking the creek. We heard from the people who lived on the other side that they recognized her as the Blessed Mother so they named her the "Lady of the Creek."

We never put a sign on our property but within a month a neighbor asked to purchase it, they even offered to let the Blessed Mother stay under the oak tree. But we brought her home. It's weather-beaten now but we still love Her and she is still on our screened porch watching over our family.

CHAPTER 23

COMFORTING CLOUDS

In January of 2005, Mary Anne, Jared and I were returning home from Jared's checkup at Numear Clinic in Jacksonville. Dr. Cyves, the wonderful surgeon who saved Jared's life, had resigned from Wolfson Hospital, thus making it difficult to locate him. Therefore, we had to keep an appointment with another doctor.

The attitude and bedside manner of the new doctor was atrocious. He was insulting about the procedure Dr. Cyves performed that saved Jared's life and was only interested in doing more surgery and making changes. Mary Anne was furious with him, and Jared left the office in tears. By the time we checked out of the clinic and got on I-95, it was pitch-black dark, and the traffic was very heavy. So, there we were, 150 miles from home with a hysterical crying child and an infuriated mother and grandmother.

I am very nervous about driving at night. As we passed through Brunswick, the traffic lessened so we were on I-95 practically alone in the cold darkness. Mary Anne, knowing how nervous I was said, "Mom, are you okay?"

I answered, "I will be okay if we can just make it to Richmond Hill because it's almost home and there's plenty of light there along the interstate."

Jared, still sobbing in the back seat of the car, leaned over my shoulder and said "Poohey (my nickname), look out the window on your side . . . look, look, it's a small cloud." It was a single white fluffy cloud about six feet around. There were no other clouds in the sky. We watched it because it was so close to the car: we felt as if we could almost touch it. It floated alongside the car for about 15 miles.

Mary Anne calmed down and said, "I wish I had my camera."

Then Jared asked, "Poohey, what do you think that is?"

I rationalized, "Well Jared, if it was a cloud we would pass by it, right?"

"Yes, ma'am,"

"Then, if it was a cloud we would go through it right?"

"Yes, ma'am," he answered.

"But it keeps moving along with the car and in front of us and appears to be leading us through the darkness."

"Then, what do you think it is," Jared inquisitively asked.

"Well, it has to be my mother, Grandmother Annie."

About that time an excited Jared yelled, "Look out the window on the other side of the car." On the passenger side near the front window was an identical fluffy cloud. "Poohey, if the first one is Granny, who do you think this one could be? Uncle Leon maybe?" he wondered.

"Well, Jared, do you remember at the doctor's office we were talking about Uncle Leon and how proud he would be of you because you were so good at cracking codes in the puzzles? So, yes, I think Uncle Leon knew how upset you were and he just came to let you know that everything is going to be okay." The two clouds suddenly changed sides for a few minutes, then changed sides again as if they were dancing. How phenomenal it was!

After all this conversation and watching both tiny clouds leading our way for about 30 miles, we approached Richmond Hill and suddenly both clouds disappeared. Remember my earlier comment: *I will not be afraid once we get to Richmond Hill because there will be plenty of light.*

In our hearts we know that those clouds were our guardian angels! Ones who love us!

CHAPTER 24

THE HEAD

It was a beautiful day in August. We had worked all day in the yards. Taking time to rest, I flopped onto the sofa. As soon as I closed my eyes, a scary vision came into my mind's eye.

I saw thick, white clouds rising upward, and then at the top of the cloud it started tapering, forming the shape of a bowl, and suddenly a head appeared in the bowl shape. When my mind's eye looked at it, I realized the head was Barry Kautz, my son-in-law's father. I was startled to see Barry.

The next morning I was so worried I called Kathleen, my daughter, to see if her father-in-law was okay. I told her what I had envisioned. She said she thought he was okay because he and his wife, Sheila, were on a cruise and would not be back till the next day. "Well, when you talk to him, tell him to be very careful."

Three days later, I got a call from Kathleen. Get this! When Barry got home from his trip, he was not feeling well so he took some medicine, which made him really dizzy. At 3 a.m. he got out of bed to use the bathroom and fell, bashing his head on the foot of the bed.

The EMS had to rush him to the hospital because his head was gushing blood. There was a big gash across his forehead and another gash across his nose between his eyes. He was in the hospital for 12 hours but is home now.

How does that vision grab you? "The head." I think my visions are back. I've been seeing lots of things lately.

CHAPTER 25

IRVIN AND ROBERTA

One Saturday night I had a vision. I could see Steve Stall in what appeared to be a funeral home chapel. He was walking alone to some empty pews. I noticed he was teary eyed. Then I saw his mother and brother walking towards me. Roberta was wearing a black dress and black hat, carrying a red rose, escorted by her other son, Mark. I felt there had been a death in their family. In my vision I saw myself take Steve by the arm and tell him to come outside for some fresh air to compose himself. Since Irvin wasn't with them I assumed the funeral was his, especially since his wife was carrying one red rose.

I was very worried but didn't want to call and tell them what I had seen. However, two days later I heard Irvin was very sick. I called Roberta and she told me that Irvin was just diagnosed with cancer and the doctors didn't expect him to live much longer. She asked "Did Steve call to tell you?"

I said, "Mark's friend had told my daughter." I didn't want to tell her my dream but I did tell her that on Saturday night I envisioned Steve was upset and I was trying to comfort him.

Roberta said, "You must have felt that Steve needed you because on Saturday night he said, 'Mom we really need to call Mildred and tell her about Dad.'"

Because Steve and I had always been close, I suppose my sixth sense came through. I could feel Steve's emotion shortly after this Irvin in my vision passed into the other world.

About two weeks later I had a phone call from Maree, my adopted "sister-cousin." She wanted to know if I would come to her house and play the Ouija Board with her daughters, Mary

Susan and Margret.

"Sure, I'll be there in a few minutes."

With my trusty old Ouija Board under my arm I hurried on over. Happily arranging our chairs together we placed our fingers on the planchet of the board. Quietly but seriously we asked, "Are there any good spirits here that would like to talk to us?"

All quiet!

Once again we asked, "Are there any good spirits that would like to talk to us? You are welcome if you are a good spirit." Suddenly, the planchet moved to the word "Yes."

We asked "What is your earthly name?" We were shocked, it spelled "Irvin."

Immediately, we asked "Do you want to tell us something?" and it spelled out, "Worried about Roberta." That was all it said and moved no more. Of course, out loud we reassured Irvin we would check on his wife and see what we could find out.

Well, we didn't want to tell Roberta we had talked to her dead husband. But we were worried about Irvin's message. Marie called her on the phone to say hello. But she was shocked when Roberta had told her she had a tumor in her breast and had been worried sick that it was cancerous. Just that day she had gotten a phone call from the doctor saying the tumor was benign. She was so relieved. Can you believe Irvin was still so worried that he wanted to let us know?

Several months later I was talking to Steve. He said his mother was in the hospital having tests done. My granddaughter Rebecca was at my house wanting to play the Ouija Board. As we started playing, who do you think came on the board? Irvin! When asked, "What do you want to tell us?" he said "Roberta is dead."

We assured him she was only in the hospital for tests. He then said, "Ruth was with him and she saw her too."

Once again we reassured him she was okay but I was so disturbed that I raced to the hospital and to her room. Very quietly I opened her door and was surprised at what I saw. She was lying in the bed, so pale and beautiful and her arms folded so sweetly across her chest. It scared me because she looked so at peace that I thought Ruth and Irvin might have been right. A nurse came in and I asked "Is Roberta all right?"

The nurse said she had been in a deep sleep from her tests but was coming out of it nicely. Relieved, I walked over to her nervously, called her name several times, and she opened her eyes and smiled. We then talked for a minute.

I came home thinking to myself, if Irvin and Ruth had gone to the hospital to see Roberta and had viewed her from above they could have thought she was dead.

Thanks a lot, Irvin, for scaring me.

CHAPTER 26

GRIM REAPER

Mary Anne dreamed she was at her old high school. The Grim Reaper, dressed all in black, walked up with a red rose in his hand. He looked at Mary Anne and shook his head to indicate "no." He turned and walked toward her friend Sharon and handed her the red rose. He then disappeared.

The next morning we were having a yard sale and Mary Anne was telling me about her dream. About that time her friends, Don and Donna, drove into the driveway. They got out of the car and very quickly walked up to Mary Anne; both put their hands on her shoulders.

Before a word was spoken Mary Anne said, "It's Sharon isn't it? She's dead!"

Stunned, Don said "How did you know? It hasn't been on the news yet." Mary Anne proceeded to tell them her dream.

Her friends said that Sharon and her fiancé were on the way to the airport to pick up his brother in her restored red Mustang. While driving down Abercorn Street a drunk driver crossed over the median and crashed into the Mustang head-on, killing her instantly.

CHAPTER 27

JOHN'S REQUEST AND LITTLE JERRY

In a dream, Mary Anne saw her deceased husband, John. He told her to check on Alan Minkovich, his life-long best friend. His request disturbed her, and she pursued his request. Mary Anne had no idea where to find Alan, so she called Kathleen, her sister, owner of Roly Poly. She told Kathleen that Alan's brother sometimes came there for a sandwich and asked her if next time he came to get Alan's phone number and address.

The next day Kathleen reported that David had come and said that Alan was in the hospital . . . in the Intensive Care Unit. He had fallen off a ladder three stories up while painting a building and suffered a broken back and other broken bones. He was a painter by trade. When Mary Anne called the hospital Alan was so happy to hear her voice but was astonished that John had told her to check on him.

Later, Alan had made a statement that he thought he was going to die because he had dreamed about John but fortunately he survived and is almost back to normal.

Little Jerry

In a vision I could see myself walking down a hospital corridor holding a little child's hand. We paused beside a patient's room, someone I must have known because, as we passed the door, I made a statement to the occupant of the room: "I'll make a prediction that he will be okay, but the doctor will want to keep him another day." Then the vision disappeared. I was concerned, wondering if the vision had any meaning. Since I had been holding a child's hand, I was afraid it might be about a child.

The next morning I called Kathleen to ask if she knew anybody in a hospital. She said she had just received a call from her daughter, Rebecca, telling her that little nephew, six-year-old Jerry, had taken ill very suddenly during the night. His parents rushed him to the hospital. Rebecca and her husband met them there.

It took a while to get his condition under control but the doctor said little Jerry would have to stay one more day.

CHAPTER 28

UNCLE GENE

Eugene Rhodes was a life-long friend and a true old-time Southern gentleman. For about 50 years we lost track of him, then with an unexplainable gift of fate, electronic airwaves helped us to be reunited. Gene was a ham radio operator for years, and so was my husband. Pete only knew Gene through radio and they talked every day, but he didn't know Gene was our old family friend. One day we went to Florida to see my sister, Ann. While there, Pete announced, "While you girls visit I think I'll go to DeLeon Springs to visit my ham buddy who used to live in Savannah. His name is Gene Rhodes."

"Oh my gosh! Did he ever work at the theaters" we asked.

"Yes," Pete replied.

When we finally were able to get together again it was a happy reunion. Gene was all alone because his mother had died. We adopted him into our family and called him Uncle Gene. Everyone loved him. He came to all the family activities: Thanksgiving, birthdays, even vacations with us to Idaho to see William, Ann's son.

He loved Jared, my grandson, and even became his Godfather. On August 17, 2005, he passed away into the other world, but he is still with us in spirit form. When Jared was very ill he gave him a fish that is mounted on the den wall and upon occasion — with no battery — the fish sings. It used to scare us but now we just say "Okay, Uncle Gene, we know you are here."

Several times his ghostly form has been seen roaming our house. Always when he came to our house he would shoot pool with Jared. Now since he passed away, on two occasions all 10 of the pool balls have mysteriously disappeared off the table, nowhere to be found in the house. Then, several days later the balls suddenly reappear in their place on the pool table.

This Thanksgiving was its usual nice family gathering, and everyone missed Uncle Gene being there. After dinner we all went to Kathleen's home to have a cocktail and sit outside around a campfire. As we sat there reminiscing about how Uncle Gene enjoyed sitting around the fire, Kathleen said, "I just got a new camera and it takes pictures in the dark." She ran to fetch it. Happy to test the night camera for the first time, she took a picture of her husband, Thomas, who was sitting by the fire holding their little dog.

Snap, Snap, Done!

She was showing the picture of Thomas and how great it turned out in the dark. When Mary Anne and Jared saw it they said at the same time, "Oh, my God, it's Uncle Gene!"

Standing next to Thomas' chair was smoke that was shaped like a man, kind of slumped just like 90-year-old Uncle Gene would stand. He even had his smoked arm around Thomas' shoulder. He and Thomas were smoking buddies when Uncle

Gene was alive.

We treasure this picture because we *know* it was Gene and he was enjoying the fire and used energy to form himself to make us know that he was with us in spirit form.

CHAPTER 29

ARE YOU A BELIEVER?

During the month of August 2007, we were under a mandatory water restriction due to the lack of rainfall and reduced water table. Early one morning we were surprised to observe a stream of water seeping out of the street in front of our house. Concerned, we notified the city's water department, which sent out a crew. The men began using jackhammers to break up the concrete under the water and then began digging to try to find the broken water line. After three days of digging, drilling, tearing up the street (and even our neighbor's driveway) they were unable to locate the source of the continuous stream of water. The only thing they could do was repair the street and driveway.

All the men in the crew were hot, tired, and exhausted. They looked so defeated. The supervisor remarked, "I can't believe we've wasted about $800 of concrete and still don't have a clue as to where the leak is coming from."

I said to the supervisor, "Sir, I think you're looking on the wrong side of the street." Of course, he laughed.

By now it was 3:00 in the afternoon and all five men were still standing in the street, bewildered. One of the older men found a piece of metal in the street that looked like an old coat hanger and went to throw it away. I stopped him and said, "Sir, if I can use that stick I can show you where the leak is."

He laughed and said, "Lady, how would you know?"

"I'm psychic."

All the men started laughing hysterically at me. As the worker handed me the metal stick I walked back to the other side of the street, on my lawn, and proceeded to use the stick as a divining rod. The rod pointed to a spot in the street next to a tree in my yard. The old man, still laughing, jokingly took a huge sledgehammer and smashed the exact spot that I marked.

Shocking the man beyond belief, water began gushing out from the street where the man smashed the concrete. At the same time, all the men yelled, "It's here, it's here!" Very quickly, the machines and shovels became active once again. The supervisor radioed for back-up crews and bulldozers. As they dug, they found that a main water pipe had been crushed by the roots of a huge pine tree, which is what caused it to rupture. They had to call the Park and Tree Commission to remove the tree before they could fix the crushed pipe.

Though it was getting very late in the evening, our whole neighborhood was outside, watching everything. Two of the men that were standing in the giant, boggy hole in the ground started laughing and one of them said, "Lady, we're glad you showed us this spot so we consider this your very own hole we're diggin'."

The crews finally completed the job around 11:00 that night. As they were packing up to leave, the man that drove the bulldozer got down and walked up to me and said, "Ma'am, can I talk to you a minute?"

"Certainly," I replied.

He said, "I'm a good Christian man and never believed in psychic things but now I am a believer. Thanks for showing us that hole. I only wish you had shown it to us yesterday."

CHAPTER 30

CONCLUSION

During my life, I have experienced many scary, spine-tingling, unbelievable experiences. We have entertained ghosts and spirits in our home and made them feel welcome only if they were good spirits. It took me years to except what God had entrusted to me.

Are you a believer?

Think about it! Have you ever experienced a strong feeling that someone was standing behind you only to turn around and find no one there? Maybe it was a spirit, a deceased family member or friend, just wanting to be near you. Or have you experienced lights blinking for no reason, radios turning on and off for no reason, or phones ringing but dead silence on the other end when you answer? Or maybe unexplained shadows? Do things disappear but later return to the exact spot where you left them?

Perhaps these mysterious occurrences are simply a deceased friend or relative trying to let you know they are still with you. Do not close your mind to the other world! Use your own psychic ability and open your mind.

Be ready. Be a believer!

I am.   ☺

Also from ThomasMax Publishing

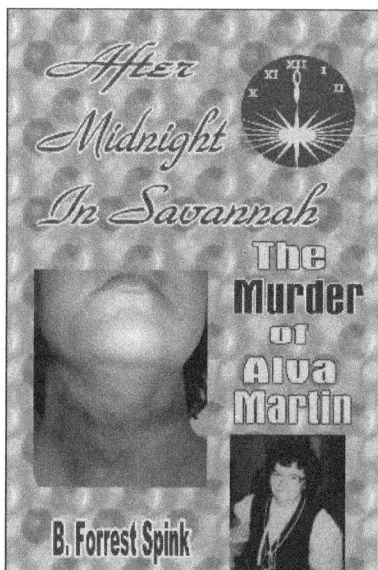

After Midnight In Savannah
By B. Forrest Spink, $ 12.95

The true story of the murder of Savannah Nazarene minister Alva Martin, whose son, Jim, was convicted of her 1991 murder. Jim Martin, a crack cocaine addict at the time of his arrest, still maintains that the killer was his drug supplier, an African-American female impersonator. Includes family photos and much of the transcript of Jim Martin's trial.

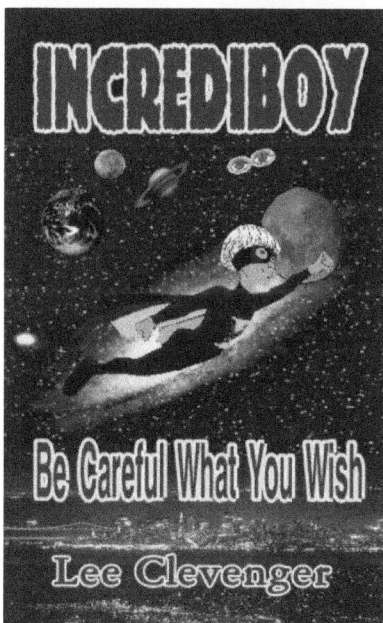

IncrediBoy: Be Careful What You Wish
By Lee Clevenger, $ 12.95

To Christian Savage, 11, life is a cruel joke. He's unpopular, unathletic and a target for bullies. Worse, his older brother is Mr. Perfect Boy. To escape life's cruelties, Christian resorts to daydreams, including his favorite of being a superhero he calls IncrediBoy. When he finds two rings lost by Yoqe, an evil alien, the power of the rings allows him to become IncrediBoy in real life. But Christian discovers that being a superhero isn't all it's cracked up to be. And Christian doesn't know it, but the evil alien is on his way back to Earth to reclaim his rings. For ages 9 & up. Includes "incrediglossary" to help younger readers build their vocabularies.

www.ingramcontent.com/pod-product-compliance
Lightning Source LLC
Chambersburg PA
CBHW032002040426
42448CB00006B/458